TIKI COCKTAILS

TIKI COCKTAILS

180+ dreamy drinks & luau-inspired libations

SHELLY SLIPSMITH

ILLUSTRATIONS BY
50s VINTAGE DAME

Smith Street Books

CONTENTS

INTRODUCTION

If you've ever had a wild night out in a tiki bar, then you have a man named Ernest Raymond Beaumont Gantt (later known as Donn Beach) to thank. A guy who cut his teeth on Prohibition-era bootlegging before traveling through the Caribbean and Pacific Islands, Gantt was inspired to open a tropical-themed cocktail bar in Los Angeles called Don the Beachcomber's in 1933. Little did he know it at the time, but he'd created the world's first tiki bar. And soon, many more would follow.

A kitschy interpretation of Polynesian culture, tiki bars have migrated from their LA birthplace to infiltrate cities all around the globe. From Paris to Seoul and beyond, these fabulous, fever dreams with nautical names and tropical decor have taken the world by storm.

Despite the incredible aesthetics of tiki bars, it really is all about the drinks. From modern cocktails given a tiki twist to old standards steeped in history, let these recipes inspire you to embrace the tiki lifestyle. Be warned though, tiki fandom can become an all-consuming hobby. One minute you're dabbling in mixing the odd Mai Tai, the next you're spending every Sunday categorizing your collection of vintage tiki mugs.

Whether you're a tried-and-true tiki veteran or simply seeking an intro to this (quite literally) intoxicating fantasy world, pull up a cane bar stool and find inspiration in these recipes from the tiki world.

GLASS TYPES

Sure, you could drink a tiki cocktail out of any old glass, but where's the fun in that? Investing in a solid collection of glassware will not only inspire you to mix drinks more often, but your cocktail parties will also be taken to the next level with your range of glorious glassware. Importantly, tiki drinks have produced their own specific mugs, glasses, bowls and vessels specific to whatever goes in it.
So honor the drink by serving it in its appropriate glass – the legends of tiki will smile on you.

Highball glass

A standard tall glass that comes in many shapes and sizes.

Old fashioned glass

A classic short cocktail glass that's sometimes called a "lowball" glass. Good for low-volume cocktails with a high alcohol content or just good old fashioned straight whiskey.

Double old fashioned glass

Much like its younger brother, only a bit bigger. As a result of its size, it holds more volume inside it.

Hurricane glass

A tall, curvaceous cocktail glass, usually with a short stem. This glass holds around 17–20 oz (500–600 ml) of delicious drink. It was named after the tiki classic Hurricane cocktail featured on page 23.

Poco grande

Similar to the hurricane glass, this curvy vessel is the more classic-shaped cocktail glass with a longer stem.

Martini glass

An elegant conical glass with a long stem, frequently spotted in the company of a white dinner jacket-wearing man from a popular series of spy movies.

Cocktail glass

A long-stemmed glass similar to a martini glass but a little smaller and often with a slightly rounded or flat bottom.

Pearl diver glass

This rather obscure glass gets its name from Donn Beach's tiki classic Pearl Diver cocktail featured on page 50. It has a straight base and curves up into a bowl at the top.

Swizzle cup

A tall and sexy metal cup that tapers out at the top. Great to freeze or pack with ice so it gets all frosty on the outside.

Metal julep cup

Similar to a swizzle cup, only shorter, this ornate silver and pewter bourbon catcher became popular at the Kentucky Derby in the 1930s.

Copper mug

The classic vessel for the Moscow Mule has a backstory. Legend has it a man was trying to sell vodka in America at a time when people weren't overly interested in drinking it. He mixed it with ginger beer and lime juice, put it in a stout copper cup and before he knew it, people all over America were drinking vodka by the gallon.

Tiki mug

These intricate ceramic mugs are the most iconic part of the tiki craze. Based on the carved wooden heads from the islands of Polynesia, Micronesia and the Pacific, these mugs were pioneered by the godfather of tiki himself, Donn Beach. Many fans have amassed huge collections of these unique vessels, such is the power of the tiki mug.

Mara Amu mug

One of the classic tiki mugs, named after a drink that originated at the Mai-Kai Restaurant in Fort Lauderdale, Florida. Get your hands on one of these mugs, then try the recipe on page 134.

Ceramic rum barrel mug

Much like its name suggests, this is a ceramic, barrel-shaped mug good for putting rum into.

Opened coconut

When you don't have the "correct" glass or mug for a cocktail, don't be afraid to improvise. There's nothing that fits the Pacific Island fantasy quite like sipping a cocktail out of a coconut. To open a coconut, first drain the water by hammering a nail into the "eyes" and then draining the liquid (mix the coconut water with rum for a great drink). Hold the coconut on its side and chop into the shell using a large sharp knife (a machete is good if you have one), turning the coconut between chops. It will take a minute or two to cut through, and be extremely careful of your fingers. Also, do this outside as bits of coconut shell can fly everywhere.

Hollowed pineapple

Another great improvised drink container. Slice the top off the pineapple, then run the knife in a circle around the inside of the skin. Cut across the core, then use a spoon to scoop out the flesh (save this for a pineapple daiquiri). Pro tip: Slice the bottom off the pineapple to stop your precious fruit vessel toppling over the second you put it down.

GARNISHES

Once you've got your beautiful cocktail in an equally beautiful glass, you need to jazz it up with a garnish. Get really creative here. Classic wheels and wedges of citrus, twisty pieces of fruit peel, dainty tropical flowers, spiky pineapple fronds, fragrant fresh herbs and novelty oversized ice cubes are all fair game.

There aren't rules when it comes to garnishes, but choose something that contrasts nicely with the color of the drink and you're onto something.

Wheel

A simple option that suits many different tiki cocktails. Place your citrus fruit of choice on its side and slice into rounds about ¼ inch (5 mm) thick. Place into your drink or cut a slit into the middle and jam it on the side of your glass. BAM! Garnished.

Slice

A standard mixed drink garnish that's straightforward to pull off. Simply cut a citrus fruit in half lengthwise, then slice into half circles. Easy.

Twist

A classy garnish that also infuses your drink with flavor. With a sharp knife, carefully separate a strip of rind from your citrus fruit of choice, discarding any pith. Trim the edges and twist the strip over the drink so that the oil in the rind sprays into the glass. Rub the twist around the rim of the glass and drop into the drink.

Wedge

Another very easy way to garnish a glass. For smallish, roundish fruit (such as citrus), cut the fruit in half and slice into wedges. Add to your drink or make a small incision in the flesh and slide onto the rim of your glass. For larger fruit (such as melon or pineapple) first cut into thick slices, then cut the slices into wedges. Cut an incision, jam that baby onto the rim of your glass and party on.

Salt or sugar rim

This garnish will also change the flavor profile of your cocktail. Run the fleshy part of some fruit around the rim of your glass. Pour some sugar or salt onto a flat plate and carefully dunk the sticky rim into the granules. Drinks that have this kind of garnish should always be sipped without a straw.

RUM-BASED

COCKTAILS

There would be no tiki without rum. But you can't just throw together a bunch of rums with some fruit juice and hope for the best. The true art of creating tiki cocktails requires both respect for the tiki tradition and some discernment with regards to the ingredients you use.

Like any recipe worth its salt, the better the ingredients you use, the better the results will be. Sure, using fresh juices and garnishes is wise, but choosing high-quality spirits is essential. White rum, dark rum, aged rum, demerara rum, French rum, Jamaican rum, Cuban rum, rum made from molasses, rum made from fresh sugar cane, over-proofed rum, navy rum, coconut rum – you'll never run out of different rums to play with.

Don't have much of a rum collection in your drinks cart? Throw a tiki party, ask your guests to each bring a different type of rum and you'll not only be able to try your hand at making some of tiki's greatest hits, you'll also be saved from the plight of having to drink them all on your lonesome. So don your loudest Hawaiian shirt, turn up the kitschy 60s tunes and get the party started with these ravishing rum recipes.

DON THE BEACHCOMBER'S MAI TAI

Both Victor Jules Bergeron (of Trader Vic's) and Ernest Raymond Gantt (aka Donn Beach of Don the Beachcomber fame) lay claim to inventing the Mai Tai. We'll likely never know the full truth, but this recipe of Donn Beach's is a good place to start your investigations.

SERVES 1

2 oz (60 ml) aged rum
⅔ oz (20 ml) orange curaçao
⅔ oz (20 ml) Orgeat syrup (page 252)
⅔ oz (20 ml) freshly squeezed lime juice
mint sprig, for garnish

Combine the ingredients (except the garnish) in a cocktail shaker with ice. Shake.

Strain into an old fashioned glass filled with crushed ice. Garnish with mint.

TRADER VIC'S MAI TAI

Trader Vic's most famous tiki cocktail uses rhum agricole (the French name for cane juice rum) instead of other rum varieties. With a more earthy flavor profile than other styles of rum, the inclusion of rhum agricole really sets this one apart from the rest.

SERVES 1

1 oz (30 ml) dark rum
1 oz (30 ml) rhum agricole (cane juice rum)
½ oz (15 ml) orange curaçao
¼ oz (7.5 ml) Orgeat syrup (page 252)
1 oz (30 ml) freshly squeezed lime juice
mint sprig, for garnish

Combine the ingredients (except the garnish) in a cocktail shaker with ice. Shake.

Strain into an old fashioned glass filled with crushed ice. Garnish with mint.

QB COOLER

A Donn Beach original that likely inspired the Mai Tai, this vintage 1930s cocktail is still going strong more than 80 years after it first appeared on the menu at Don the Beachcomber.

SERVES 1

1 oz (30 ml) gold rum
1 oz (30 ml) white rum
½ oz (15 ml) demerara rum
⅓ oz (10 ml) ginger liqueur
1 oz (30 ml) freshly squeezed orange juice
½ oz (15 ml) freshly squeezed lime juice
½ oz (15 ml) Honey syrup (page 253)
¼ oz (7.5 ml) Velvet falernum (page 257)
1 oz (30 ml) soda water
2 dashes Orange bitters (page 258)
mint sprig, for garnish

Place the ingredients (except the garnish) in a high-speed blender with ½ cup crushed ice. Blend at high speed for 5 seconds.

Pour into a large old fashioned glass and top with crushed ice. Garnish with mint.

DRAGON 88 MAI TAI

You might not associate West Boylston, Massachusetts with tiki culture, but a suburban Chinese restaurant in this unlikely corner of the USA created a Mai Tai worthy of traveling for. This variation of the restaurant's recipe is more complex than an original recipe Mai Tai, but equally as delicious.

SERVES 1

1½ oz (45 ml) rhum agricole (cane juice rum)
1 oz (30 ml) demerara rum
1 oz (30 ml) dark spiced rum
½ oz (15 ml) orange curaçao
½ oz (15 ml) freshly squeezed lime juice
½ oz (15 ml) Orgeat syrup (page 252)
½ oz (15 ml) Velvet falernum (page 257)
pineapple wedge and maraschino cherry, for garnish

Combine the ingredients (except the garnish) in a cocktail shaker with ice. Shake.

Strain into an old fashioned glass filled with crushed ice. Garnish with a pineapple wedge with a maraschino cherry and a straw.

BITTER MAI TAI

If you like your tipples on the tarter side of life, get acquainted with this beautifully bitter version of the Mai Tai. The perfect pre-dinner sip, serve this one as an aperitif to start your next dinner party.

SERVES 1

1 oz (30 ml) dark rum
1½ oz (45 ml) Campari
½ oz (15 ml) orange curaçao
1 oz (30 ml) freshly squeezed lime juice
⅔ oz (20 ml) Orgeat syrup (page 252)
mint sprig, for garnish

Combine the ingredients (except the garnish) in a cocktail shaker filled with ice. Shake.

Strain into an old fashioned glass filled with crushed ice. Garnish with mint.

HURRICANE

Created to use up excess
rum, this potent drink was
first mixed in a New Orleans
speakeasy back in the 1940 s.
Proving popular with sailors,
the Hurricane stuck around to become a mainstay
on the cocktail scene. Just like the resilient city it was
birthed in; the Hurricane is a real stayer.

SERVES 1

2 oz (60 ml) white rum
2 oz (60 ml) dark rum
1 oz (30 ml) freshly squeezed lime juice
1 oz (30 ml) freshly squeezed orange juice
2 oz (60 ml) passionfruit pulp
½ oz (15 ml) Passionfruit syrup (page 256)
½ oz (15 ml) Sugar syrup (page 250)
½ oz (15 ml) Grenadine (page 251)
⅙ oz (5 ml) Orgeat syrup (page 252)
orange wheel and maraschino cherry, for garnish

Combine the ingredients (except the garnish) in a cocktail
shaker with ice. Shake.

Strain into a hurricane glass filled with ice. Garnish with
an orange wheel and maraschino cherry.

For an extra kick, finish the drink with over-proofed
rum floated on top.

NAVY GROG

*If you're a purist, you'll need to invest some
time into making this Donn Beach original. Preparing
the fiddly snow cone garnish a few hours ahead
might require a bit of foresight (and a freezer),
but Donn Beach would salute your efforts.*

SERVES 1

1 oz (30 ml) dark rum
1 oz (30 ml) demerara rum
1 oz (30 ml) white rum
⅔ oz (20 ml) freshly squeezed lime juice
⅔ oz (20 ml) freshly squeezed grapefruit juice
1 oz (30 ml) Honey syrup (page 253)
1 oz (30 ml) soda water
lime wedge, for garnish

Combine the rums, fruit juices and honey syrup in
a cocktail shaker filled with ice. Shake.

Strain into an old fashioned glass filled with crushed ice.
Top with the soda water and garnish with a lime wedge.

*Traditionally this drink is garnished with a frozen "snow cone"
with a straw through the middle. You can make your own by
filling a cone-shaped glass with finely crushed ice, poking
a straw through the center and freezing it for a few hours.*

COLONIAL GROG

A Donn Beach recipe that has been revisited and reinvented by tiki historian Jeff "Beachbum" Berry, the addition of maple syrup gives this delicious cocktail a rich, slightly buttery texture.

SERVES 1

½ oz (15 ml) dark rum
½ oz (15 ml) gold rum
½ oz (15 ml) freshly squeezed lime juice
½ oz (15 ml) freshly squeezed orange juice
½ oz (15 ml) soda water
⅓ oz (10 ml) maple syrup
⅙ oz (5 ml) Allspice dram (page 259)
1 dash Orange bitters (page 258)
orange wheel, for garnish

Place the ingredients (except the garnish) in a high-speed blender with ½ cup crushed ice. Blend at high speed for 5 seconds.

Strain into an old fashioned glass filled with crushed ice. Garnish with an orange wheel.

Traditionally, this drink is served in a glass lined with a shell of crushed ice. To do this, fill an old fashioned glass with finely crushed ice. With a spoon, slowly create a well in the middle, pushing the ice up the side of the glass. When you have a well in the ice, put the glass in the freezer for a few hours before serving.

COFFEE GROG

A rum-toddy tipple to fuel a night of work or play, this caffeinated cocktail is perfectly acceptable to enjoy at breakfast too. Serve with a side of pancakes for the ultimate hair-of-the-dog culinary experience.

SERVES 1

½ teaspoon sugar
⅙ oz (5 ml) Coffee grog batter (page 261)
1 pinch ground nutmeg
1 pinch ground cloves
1 pinch ground cinnamon
3 strips orange rind
1 strip grapefruit rind
6 oz (180 ml) freshly brewed coffee
½ oz (15 ml) aged rum
½ oz (15 ml) 151 proof dark rum
cinnamon stick, for garnish

Place the sugar, batter, spices and rind in a large warmed mug or heatproof glass. Pour in the hot coffee and stir until the sugar is dissolved.

Combine the rums in a metal ladle or small heatproof jug and carefully ignite. Pour the flaming rum into the coffee mixture and garnish with a cinnamon stick.

PLANTER'S PUNCH

A wine-glass with lemon juice fill,
Of sugar the same glass fill twice
Then rub them together until
The mixture looks smooth, soft, and nice.

Of rum then three wine glasses add,
And four of cold water please take.
A Drink then you'll have that's not bad
At least, so they say in Jamaica.

– Fun Magazine, September, 1878

Make like Humphrey Bogart in the 1942 adventure flick
Across the Pacific and order this fruity classic associated
with South Carolina's iconic Planters Inn.

SERVES 1

1½ oz (45 ml) dark rum
1 oz (30 ml) white rum
1 oz (30 ml) freshly squeezed lemon juice
1 oz (30 ml) Honey syrup (page 253)
2 dashes Orange bitters (page 258)
2 oz (60 ml) soda water
mint sprig, pineapple wedge and
maraschino cherry, for garnish

Combine the rums, lemon juice, honey syrup and
bitters in a cocktail shaker filled with ice. Shake.

Strain into a large glass filled with ice cubes.
Top with the soda and garnish with mint,
a pineapple wedge and maraschino cherry.

TIKI SWIZZLE

Much more than a stirring implement, a cocktail drinking session is instantly made much more fun by the addition of a novelty swizzle stick.

SERVES 1

1½ oz (45 ml) spiced rum

⅔ oz (20 ml) dark rum

½ oz (15 ml) freshly squeezed lime juice

½ oz (15 ml) Passionfruit syrup (page 256)

½ oz (15 ml) Sugar syrup (page 250)

2 dashes Orange bitters (page 258)

passionfruit pulp and pineapple wedge, for garnish

Place the ingredients (except the garnish) in a high-speed blender with 1 cup crushed ice. Blend at high speed for 5 seconds.

Pour into a chilled swizzle or other stainless steel cup and top with crushed ice. Garnish with a swizzle stick, passionfruit pulp and a pineapple wedge.

ZOMBIE

A trifecta of different rum varieties forms the basis of this lethal Donn Beach original that's guaranteed to get the party started. If you need to resurrect the dead, pour a few Zombies.

SERVES 1

1½ oz (45 ml) gold rum

1½ oz (45 ml) dark rum

1 oz (30 ml) 151 proof demerara rum

⅔ oz (20 ml) freshly squeezed lime juice

½ oz (15 ml) Velvet falernum (page 257)

⅙ oz (5 ml) Grenadine (page 251)

⅙ oz (5 ml) Pernod

1 dash Orange bitters (page 258)

½ oz (15 ml) Don's mix (page 261)

mint sprig, for garnish

Place the ingredients (except the garnish) in a high-speed blender with ¾ cup crushed ice. Blend at high speed for 5 seconds.

Pour into a highball glass and top up with ice cubes. Garnish with mint and drink responsibly.

CLASSIC DAIQUIRI

Whoever first mixed rum, sugar and lime together was onto something – this classic Cuban tipple is a reliable favorite featured on cocktail menus from Havana to Honolulu, Helsinki and beyond.

SERVES 1

2 oz (60 ml) white rum
1 oz (30 ml) freshly squeezed lime juice
½ oz (15 ml) Sugar syrup (page 250)
lime wheel, for garnish

Combine the ingredients (except the garnish) in a cocktail shaker filled with ice. Shake.

Strain into a chilled cocktail glass and garnish with a lime wheel.

PINEAPPLE DAIQUIRI

Amp up the tropical vibes of your Daiquiri by infusing it with pineapple to create this fruity version that's pretty much an island vacation in a glass.

SERVES 1

2¾ oz (½ cup) chopped fresh pineapple
5 mint leaves
2 oz (60 ml) pineapple rum
1 oz (30 ml) freshly squeezed lime juice
½ oz (15 ml) Sugar syrup (page 250)
pineapple wedge, for garnish

Muddle the pineapple and mint in a cocktail shaker. Add the rum, lime and sugar syrup and fill the shaker with ice. Shake vigorously.

Strain into a chilled cocktail glass. Garnish with a pineapple wedge.

STRAWBERRY DAIQUIRI

Fresh, fruity, fun and packed with flavor, this smooth, strawberry blended cocktail is synonymous with summer.

SERVES 1

9 oz (250 g) strawberries, hulled and cut in half
2 oz (¼ cup) sugar
1 oz (30 ml) freshly squeezed lemon juice
2 oz (60 ml) white rum
⅔ oz (20 ml) strawberry liqueur (optional)
⅔ oz (20 ml) freshly squeezed lime juice
⅔ oz (20 ml) Sugar syrup (page 250)
lime wheel and strawberries, for garnish

In a small bowl, combine the strawberries with the sugar and lemon juice. Cover and refrigerate for 30 minutes.

Place the strawberries in a high-speed blender with the rest of the ingredients (except the garnish) and 1 cup ice. Blend at high speed until smooth.

Pour into a large cocktail glass and garnish with a lime wheel and sliced strawberries.

FROZEN LIME DAIQUIRI

On a sizzling summer's day, nothing beats a frozen cocktail. This super-refreshing lime number will quench your thirst and put you into relaxation mode in no time.

SERVES 1

3 oz (90 ml) white rum
2 oz (60 ml) freshly squeezed lime juice
1 oz (30 ml) Sugar syrup (page 250)
lime wheel, for garnish

Place the ingredients (except the garnish) in a high-speed blender with 1 cup ice. Blend at high speed until smooth.

Pour into a large cocktail glass and garnish with a lime wheel.

MANGO DAIQUIRI

If you're blessed to live in an area with an abundance of mangoes (or even better, happen to have a mango tree in your yard) then it's your duty to make (and drink) as many of these smooth-as-silk Daiquiris as possible.

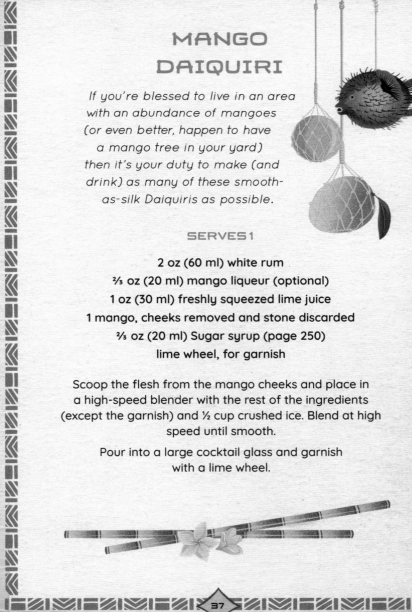

SERVES 1

2 oz (60 ml) white rum
⅔ oz (20 ml) mango liqueur (optional)
1 oz (30 ml) freshly squeezed lime juice
1 mango, cheeks removed and stone discarded
⅔ oz (20 ml) Sugar syrup (page 250)
lime wheel, for garnish

Scoop the flesh from the mango cheeks and place in a high-speed blender with the rest of the ingredients (except the garnish) and ½ cup crushed ice. Blend at high speed until smooth.

Pour into a large cocktail glass and garnish with a lime wheel.

BAHAMA MAMA

*If you think dark rum, white rum and coconut rum
is a lot of alcohol, then wait for the late arrival of
the 151 proof rum to hit your palate once you get
toward the bottom of this serious cocktail.*

SERVES 1

1 oz (30 ml) dark rum
½ oz (15 ml) white rum
½ oz (15 ml) coconut rum
3 oz (90 ml) pineapple juice, fresh if possible
2 oz (60 ml) freshly squeezed orange juice
1 oz (30 ml) freshly squeezed lemon juice
1 dash Orange bitters (page 258)
⅙ oz (5 ml) Grenadine (page 251)
½ oz (15 ml) 151 proof rum
**pineapple wedge, orange wheel and maraschino cherry,
for garnish**

Combine the dark, white and coconut rums with the fruit juices
and bitters in a cocktail shaker filled with ice. Shake.

Strain into a poco grande or other tall glass filled with ice.

Add the grenadine, pouring it slowly down the side of the glass
(it should sink to the bottom). Float the 151 proof rum on top by
pouring it over the back of a spoon.

Garnish with a pineapple wedge, orange wheel and maraschino
cherry, and drink through a straw.

TIKI-TI
FIVE-O

A heady, zingy homage to the early days of tiki, Jeff "Beachbum" Berry created this tipple to celebrate 50 years of Tiki-Ti, a landmark Los Angeles tiki bar that's been a stalwart on the scene since the 60s.

SERVES 1

2 oz (60 ml) aged rum
1 oz (30 ml) Honey syrup (page 253)
1 oz (30 ml) freshly squeezed lime juice
½ oz (15 ml) freshly squeezed orange juice
⅓ oz (10 ml) ginger liqueur
1 pinch Chinese five-spice, plus extra for garnish
lime wheel and candied ginger, for garnish

Combine the ingredients (except the garnish) in a cocktail shaker filled with ice. Shake.

Pour the contents of the shaker into a highball glass. Garnish with five-spice, a lime wheel and candied ginger.

BEACHCOMBER

*After a long, hot day walking on
soft sand, retreat to your beach bar
and mix up this citrusy take on
Donn Beach's Daiquiri.*

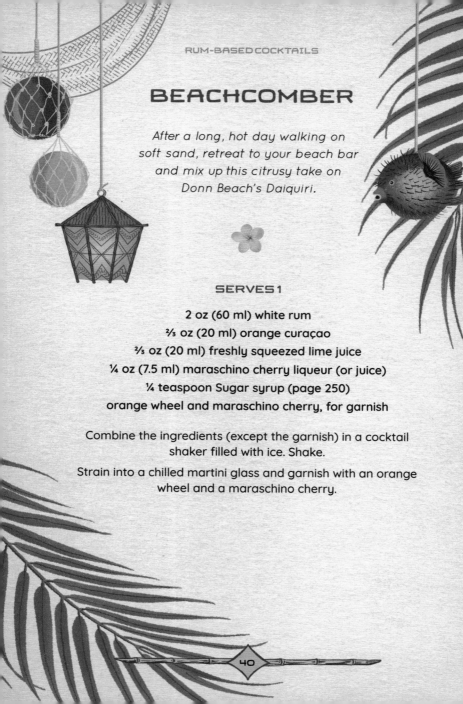

SERVES 1

2 oz (60 ml) white rum
⅔ oz (20 ml) orange curaçao
⅔ oz (20 ml) freshly squeezed lime juice
¼ oz (7.5 ml) maraschino cherry liqueur (or juice)
¼ teaspoon Sugar syrup (page 250)
orange wheel and maraschino cherry, for garnish

Combine the ingredients (except the garnish) in a cocktail
shaker filled with ice. Shake.

Strain into a chilled martini glass and garnish with an orange
wheel and a maraschino cherry.

PAINKILLER

A cocktail created by a company that makes a potent, 54% ABV rum using the original Royal Navy recipe, is a cocktail that means business.

SERVES 1

2–3 oz (60–90 ml) aged rum

4 oz (120 ml) pineapple juice, fresh if possible

1 oz (30 ml) freshly squeezed orange juice

½ oz (15 ml) coconut cream

½ oz (15 ml) Sugar syrup (page 250)

pineapple wedge, maraschino cherry and freshly grated nutmeg, for garnish

Combine the ingredients (except the garnish) in a cocktail shaker filled with ice. Shake.

Strain into an old fashioned glass filled with crushed ice. Garnish with a pineapple wedge, a maraschino cherry and freshly grated nutmeg.

THE ANCIENT MARINER

Another Jeff "Beachbum" Berry creation, this cocktail came to life when he was experimenting with ingredients while attempting to crack the code of Donn Beach's Navy Grog. He didn't succeed in his original mission, but he made this pretty nifty drink instead.

SERVES 1

1 oz (30 ml) demerara rum
1 oz (30 ml) dark rum
⅔ oz (20 ml) freshly squeezed lime juice
½ oz (15 ml) freshly squeezed grapefruit juice
½ oz (15 ml) Sugar syrup (page 250)
¼ oz (7.5 ml) Allspice dram (page 259)
mint sprig and lime wedge, for garnish

Combine the ingredients (except the garnish) in a cocktail shaker filled with ice. Shake.

Pour the contents of the shaker into a tiki mug or old fashioned glass and top up with more ice if necessary.

Garnish with mint and a lime wedge.

PAMPANITO

A modern tiki recipe from San Francisco's favorite rum-den Smuggler's Cove, the addition of molasses gives this cocktail real depth and sweetness.

SERVES 1

1½ oz (45 ml) aged rum
1 oz (30 ml) freshly squeezed lemon juice
½ oz (15 ml) light molasses
½ oz (15 ml) Sugar syrup (page 250)
¼ oz (7.5 ml) Allspice dram (page 259)
1 dash Orange bitters (page 258)
3 oz (90 ml) soda water
lemon twist, for garnish

Combine the rum, lemon juice, molasses, sugar syrup, allspice dram and bitters in a cocktail shaker filled with ice. Shake.

Strain into a highball glass filled with ice, top with the soda water and stir. Garnish with a lemon twist.

WICKED WAHINE

Cocktail appreciator Brice Ginardi created this drink after finding the West Coast tiki bar trend hadn't found its way to Hawaii. So he opened a bar in Kailua-Kona, where this taste of summer proved a winner.

SERVES 1

1½ oz (45 ml) spiced rum

¼ oz (7.5 ml) Velvet falernum (page 257)

¼ oz (7.5 ml) freshly squeezed lemon juice

¼ oz (7.5 ml) freshly squeezed lime juice

¼ oz (7.5 ml) Passionfruit syrup (page 256)

¼ oz (7.5 ml) Grenadine (page 251)

1 dash Orange bitters (page 258)

edible flower, for garnish

Combine the ingredients (except the garnish) in a cocktail shaker filled with ice. Shake.

Strain into a chilled cocktail glass and garnish with an edible flower.

VICIOUS VIRGIN

This smooth, blended cocktail served in a champagne flute may have the word "virgin" in its name, but with the inclusion of white and dark rum, it's definitely not for teetotallers.

SERVES 1

½ oz (15 ml) dark rum

1 oz (30 ml) white rum

¼ oz (7.5 ml) Velvet falernum (page 257)

½ oz (15 ml) orange curaçao

⅔ oz (20 ml) freshly squeezed lime juice

maraschino cherry, for garnish

Place the ingredients (except the garnish) in a high-speed blender with ½ cup ice and blend until smooth.

Pour into a chilled champagne flute. Garnish with a maraschino cherry.

NEVER SAY DIE

*When you're not ready to say
the night is over, mix up one of these
drinks infused with a triple treat of
rum varieties and four different types
of zesty citrus. No retreat.
No surrender.*

SERVES 1

1 oz (30 ml) aged rum
½ oz (15 ml) white rum
½ oz (15 ml) dark rum
½ oz (15 ml) freshly squeezed lime juice
½ oz (15 ml) freshly squeezed orange juice
½ oz (15 ml) pineapple juice, fresh if possible
½ oz (15 ml) Honey syrup (page 253)
1 dash Orange bitters (page 258)
pink grapefruit slice, for garnish

Place the ingredients (except the garnish) in a high-speed blender with ½ cup crushed ice. Blend at high speed for 5 seconds.

Pour into an old fashioned glass and top with crushed ice.

Garnish with a pink grapefruit slice.

TANGAROA

Mango and amaretto might not seem like obvious bedfellows, but this Beachbum Berry creation named after the god of the ocean is an understated choice for discerning cocktail aficionados.

SERVES 1

1 oz (30 ml) white rum
1 oz (30 ml) gold rum
¼ oz (7.5 ml) amaretto
2 oz (60 ml) mango nectar
½ oz (15 ml) freshly squeezed lime juice
cinnamon stick, for garnish

Combine the ingredients (except the garnish) in a cocktail shaker filled with ice. Shake.

Strain into a chilled champagne flute and garnish with a cinnamon stick.

POLYNESIAN PEARL DIVER

Another curious creation from the mind of tiki godfather Donn Beach, you'll need butter (yes, butter) to make this decadent delight. If you're keen to stay true to the original, you'll also need to procure the special glass it's traditionally served in.

SERVES 1

1½ oz (45 ml) white rum

½ oz (15 ml) demerara rum

½ oz (15 ml) dark rum

⅙ oz (5 ml) Velvet falernum (page 257)

1 oz (30 ml) freshly squeezed orange juice

⅔ oz (20 ml) Pearl diver's mix (page 260)

pearl diver glass or opened coconut, for serving (optional)

pineapple leaf and edible flower, for garnish

Place the ingredients (except the garnish) in a high-speed blender with 1 cup crushed ice. Blend at high speed until smooth.

Pour into a pearl diver glass or coconut and garnish with a pineapple leaf and an edible flower.

DEMERARA DRY FLOAT

Featuring demerara rum from Guyana in South America, you'll be floating on cloud nine after sipping a few of these.

SERVES 1

1 oz (30 ml) demerara rum
1 oz (30 ml) freshly squeezed lime juice
¼ oz (7.5 ml) freshly squeezed lemon juice
½ oz (15 ml) Passionfruit syrup (page 256)
¼ oz (7.5 ml) maraschino cherry liqueur (or juice)
½ oz (15 ml) 151 proof demerara rum
maraschino cherry, for garnish

Combine the demerara rum, fruit juices, passionfruit syrup and cherry liqueur in a cocktail shaker filled with ice. Shake.

Strain into a large old fashioned glass filled with crushed ice. Carefully float the 151 proof rum on top by pouring it over the back of a spoon.

Garnish with a maraschino cherry and drink through a straw.

QUEEN'S ROAD COCKTAIL

This under-the-radar Donn Beach recipe is often overshadowed by his more famous creations. But if you love a bit of a ginger kick in your drinks, then take a stroll down Queen's Road.

SERVES 1

1½ oz (45 ml) gold rum
⅙ oz (5 ml) ginger liqueur
½ oz (15 ml) freshly squeezed lime juice
½ oz (15 ml) freshly squeezed orange juice
½ oz (15 ml) Honey syrup (page 253)
1 dash Orange bitters (page 258)
orange twist, for garnish

Combine the ingredients (except the garnish) in a cocktail shaker filled with ice. Shake.

Strain into a chilled cocktail glass. Garnish with an orange twist.

CUBA LIBRE

Translating to "Free Cuba", this drink's origins can be traced back to the Spanish-American war of the early 20th century. Representing much more than just rum and cola with a bit of lime, make this cocktail with Cuban rum to ensure authenticity.

SERVES 1

1½ oz (45 ml) dark Cuban rum
1 oz (30 ml) freshly squeezed lime juice
2 oz (60 ml) cola
lime wedge, for garnish

Combine the ingredients (except the garnish) in a highball glass filled with crushed ice and stir to combine.

Garnish with a lime wedge.

TAHITIAN BREEZE

Just as the name suggests, this sublime, sunset-colored cocktail is as fresh as a light breeze coming in off a Polynesian beach.

SERVES 1

1 oz (30 ml) white rum

1 oz (30 ml) gold rum

1 oz (30 ml) freshly squeezed pink grapefruit juice

1 oz (30 ml) freshly squeezed orange juice

½ oz (15 ml) Passionfruit syrup (page 256)

passionfruit pulp and pink grapefruit wheel, for garnish

Place the ingredients (except the garnish) in a high-speed blender with crushed ice. Blend at high speed for 5 seconds.

Pour into a highball glass. Float the passionfruit pulp on top and garnish with a grapefruit wheel.

NUI NUI

Years of investigations led tiki aficionado Jeff "Beachbum" Berry to pin down the secret ingredients of this Donn Beach original. The mix of spices, vanilla and cinnamon syrup make this the perfect cocktail to serve at Christmas.

SERVES 1

2 oz (60 ml) gold rum
½ oz (15 ml) freshly squeezed lime juice
½ oz (15 ml) freshly squeezed orange juice
¼ oz (7.5 ml) Cinnamon syrup (page 255)
⅙ oz (5 ml) Allspice dram (page 259)
⅙ oz (5 ml) Vanilla syrup (page 254)
1 dash Orange bitters (page 258)
orange twist, for garnish

Place the ingredients (except the garnish) in a high-speed blender with 1 cup crushed ice. Blend at high speed for 5 seconds.

Pour into a tiki mug and top with crushed ice. Garnish with an orange twisted straw.

ROYAL CANADIAN KILTED YAKSMAN

You don't need to hail from the north to appreciate a cocktail spiked with maple syrup. A highball glass of this concoction will have you speaking like a Canadian in no time, eh?

SERVES 1

1 oz (30 ml) spiced rum
1 oz (30 ml) dark rum
⅓ oz (10 ml) Cinnamon syrup (page 255)
⅓ oz (10 ml) maple syrup
1 oz (30 ml) freshly squeezed lime juice
2 oz (60 ml) ginger beer
cinnamon stick, for garnish

Place the rums, syrups and lime juice in a high-speed blender with 1 cup crushed ice. Blend at high speed for 5 seconds.

Pour into a highball glass and top with more crushed ice. Top with the ginger beer.

Garnish with a cinnamon stick.

FEDERALI

Turned off by sugary cocktails? This recipe achieves the perfect balance between sweet and sour through the addition of both agave syrup and fresh lemon juice.

SERVES 1

1 oz (30 ml) white rum
1 oz (30 ml) aged rum
⅓ oz (10 ml) agave syrup
⅓ oz (10 ml) Orgeat syrup (page 252)
1 oz (30 ml) freshly squeezed lemon juice
orange wheel, for garnish

Combine the ingredients (except the garnish) in a cocktail shaker filled with ice. Shake.

Strain into an old fashioned glass filled with crushed ice. Garnish with an orange wheel.

PIÑA COLADA

An all-time favorite on the tropical resort circuit, this creamy, coconut-heavy fruit bomb was also immortalized by a late-70s one hit wonder. Decades later, it's still hard to drink one without breaking out into song.

SERVES 1

1 oz (30 ml) gold rum
1 oz (30 ml) white rum
1⅔ oz (50 ml) coconut milk
1⅓ oz (40 ml) Sugar syrup (page 250)
2⅔ oz (80 ml) pineapple juice, fresh if possible
⅔ oz (20 ml) freshly squeezed lime juice
½ oz (15 ml) heavy (double) cream
pineapple wedge and leaf, maraschino cherry
and cocktail umbrella, for garnish

Place the ingredients (except the garnish) in a high-speed blender with 1 cup ice. Pulse until the ice is crushed.

Pour into a poco grande or other tall glass and garnish with a pineapple wedge and leaf, maraschino cherry and cocktail umbrella.

DARK AND STORMY

A gateway drink that's a perfect introduction to the many wonders of rum. Mix one of these for that friend who claims they don't like rum and you might just convert them.

SERVES 1

1½ oz (45 ml) dark rum

1 oz (30 ml) freshly squeezed lime juice

2 dashes Orange bitters (page 258)

2 oz (60 ml) ginger beer

lime wedge, for garnish

Combine the ingredients (except the garnish) in a highball glass filled with crushed ice and stir to combine.

Garnish with a lime wedge.

VIEQUENSE

A simple cocktail that's easy to make and even easier to drink, whip this up when you're in the mood for a taste of the Caribbean, without complications.

SERVES 1

2 oz (60 ml) dark rum

1 oz (30 ml) amaretto

2 oz (60 ml) freshly squeezed orange juice

2 oz (60 ml) coconut cream

orange wheel and maraschino cherry, for garnish

Combine the ingredients (except the garnish) in a cocktail shaker filled with ice. Shake.

Strain into a highball glass filled with ice. Garnish with an orange wheel and a maraschino cherry.

ORANGE WHIP

The 80s cult flick The Blues Brothers *is responsible for this cocktail's rise to fame. Just one improvised line uttered by John Candy and people are still ordering this citrusy drink decades later. Now, who wants an Orange Whip?*

SERVES 1

1 oz (30 ml) white rum
1 oz (30 ml) dark rum
½ oz (15 ml) orange curaçao
1 oz (30 ml) freshly squeezed lime juice
1½ oz (45 ml) freshly squeezed orange juice
⅙ oz (5 ml) Grenadine (page 251)
orange wheel, for garnish

Place the ingredients (except the garnish) in a high-speed blender with 1 cup ice and blend at high speed until smooth.

Pour into a cocktail glass. Garnish with an orange wheel.

THE FLAMING WISDOM OF PELE

A fiery liquid tribute to the Hawaiian goddess of the volcano, you'll certainly ignite the night when you bring this complex cocktail to life.

SERVES 1

1 oz (30 ml) 151 proof rum, plus extra for garnish

1 oz (30 ml) dark rum

1 oz (30 ml) white rum

½ oz (15 ml) aged rum

⅔ oz (20 ml) freshly squeezed lime juice (reserve 1 squeezed lime half for garnish)

⅔ oz (20 ml) freshly squeezed grapefruit juice

⅔ oz (20 ml) Velvet falernum (page 257)

½ oz (15 ml) Honey syrup (page 253)

¼ oz (7.5 ml) Cinnamon syrup (page 255)

2 dashes Orange bitters (page 258)

Combine the ingredients (except the reserved lime half) in a cocktail shaker filled with ice. Shake.

Strain into a tiki mug or highball glass filled with crushed ice.

Invert the reserved lime half so that the skin side creates a cup. Place in the top of the drink.

Fill the lime cup with extra 151 proof rum and carefully ignite. After 15 seconds, blow out the flame and tip the rum into the drink.

TEST PILOT

Donn Beach created this one in the early 1940s as aviators took to the skies in World War Two. It will only take one or two of these for your night to truly take off.

SERVES 1

1½ oz (45 ml) dark rum

⅔ oz (20 ml) white rum

⅓ oz (10 ml) orange curaçao

⅙ oz (5 ml) Pernod

½ oz (15 ml) freshly squeezed lime juice

½ oz (15 ml) Velvet falernum (page 257)

1 dash Orange bitters (page 258)

orange wheel, for garnish

Place the ingredients (except the garnish) in a high-speed blender with 1 cup ice. Blend at high speed until smooth.

Pour into a large cocktail glass and garnish with an orange wheel.

CRADLE OF LIFE

Part-cocktail, part-pyrotechnic display, this fiery cocktail is a real showstopper. Just as humans sat around the campfire eons ago, watch a crowd gather around when you light this baby up!

SERVES 1

1 oz (30 ml) aged rum

1 oz (30 ml) spiced rum

½ oz (15 ml) freshly squeezed lemon juice

½ oz (15 ml) freshly squeezed lime juice
(reserve 1 squeezed lime half for garnish)

½ oz (15 ml) freshly squeezed orange juice

½ oz (15 ml) Orgeat syrup (page 252)

1⁄12 oz (2.5 ml) Orange bitters (page 258)

½ lime

⅓ oz (10 ml) green chartreuse

Combine the rums, fruit juices, syrup and bitters in a cocktail shaker (no ice). Shake.

Strain into an old fashioned glass filled with crushed ice.

Invert the reserved lime half so that the skin side creates a cup. Place in the top of the drink.

Fill the lime cup with green chartreuse and carefully ignite. After 15 seconds, blow out the flame and tip the chartreuse into the drink.

JET PILOT

Inspired by Donn Beach's Test Pilot (page 67), this spicy creation was reportedly first made in the late 1950s and soon found itself flying high in tiki bars across the world.

SERVES 1

1 oz (30 ml) dark rum
⅔ oz (20 ml) white rum
⅔ oz (20 ml) 151 proof demerara rum
⅙ oz (5 ml) Pernod
½ oz (15 ml) freshly squeezed grapefruit juice
½ oz (15 ml) freshly squeezed lime juice
½ oz (15 ml) Cinnamon syrup (page 255)
1 dash Orange bitters (page 258)
maraschino cherry, for garnish

Place the ingredients (except the garnish) in a high-speed blender with 1 cup ice. Blend at high speed until smooth.

Pour into a large cocktail glass and garnish with a maraschino cherry.

THE NIGHT MARCHER

This cocktail with a fiery bite was a signature drink at Los Angeles haunt, the Tar Pit. Even though the bar is now closed, you can still enjoy a taste of LA by creating this cocktail that hangs its hat on a hit of hot sauce.

SERVES 1

2⅔ oz (80 ml) aged rum
½ oz (15 ml) 151 proof rum
½ oz (15 ml) green chartreuse
⅔ oz (20 ml) freshly squeezed lime juice
⅔ oz (20 ml) Demerara sugar syrup (page 250)
1 dash hot sauce
2 dashes Orange bitters (page 258)
2 oz (60 ml) ginger beer
lime wedge and candied ginger, for garnish

Place the liquor, lime juice, sugar syrup, hot sauce and bitters in a highball glass. Stir well to combine.

Fill the glass with crushed ice and top with the ginger beer. Garnish with a lime wedge and candied ginger.

COCONUT RUM

*Inject some tropical vacation vibes into
your next get together with this sugary, minty,
coconutty delight. Serve it in a coconut shell
for added effect (and less washing
up at the end of the night).*

SERVES 1

1 oz (30 ml) white rum
1 oz (30 ml) dark rum
½ oz (15 ml) coconut rum
1 oz (30 ml) freshly squeezed lime juice
1 handful mint leaves, chopped
2 oz (60 ml) coconut water
½ oz (15 ml) Orgeat syrup (page 252)
½ oz (15 ml) Sugar syrup (page 250)
opened coconut, for serving (optional)
3 oz (90 ml) ginger beer
pineapple wedge and cocktail umbrella, for garnish

Combine the rums, lime juice, mint, coconut water and
syrups in a cocktail shaker filled with ice. Shake.

Strain into a coconut (or a large cocktail glass) filled
with crushed ice and top with the ginger beer.

Garnish with a pineapple wedge and cocktail umbrella.

RUM JULEP

*What happens when
Donn Beach decides to reinvent
the classic Kentucky Derby cocktail?
You get this memorable,
herbaceous tipple that
surprisingly doesn't
feature any mint.*

SERVES 1

1½ oz (45 ml) demerara rum
½ oz (15 ml) aged rum
½ oz (15 ml) freshly squeezed lime juice
½ oz (15 ml) freshly squeezed orange juice
½ oz (15 ml) Honey syrup (page 253)
¼ teaspoon Grenadine (page 251)
¼ teaspoon Velvet falernum (page 257)
¼ teaspoon Allspice dram (page 259)
1 dash Orange bitters (page 258)

Place the ingredients (except the garnish) in a high-speed blender with ½ cup crushed ice. Blend at high speed for 5 seconds.

Pour into a metal julep cup or highball glass and top with crushed ice.

MYSTERY GARDENIA

After you've perfected the usual tiki suspects, try creating this unusual drink. Two teaspoons of unsalted butter give this drink a luxurious rich texture, while the honey adds a hint of sweetness. Get the balance right and you'll have plenty of fans lining up for more.

SERVES 1

⅓ oz (10 ml) honey, warmed

⅓ oz (10 ml) unsalted butter, softened

1½ oz (45 ml) white rum

½ oz (15 ml) freshly squeezed lime juice

1 dash Orange bitters (page 258)

mint sprig, for garnish

In a small bowl, whip the honey and butter together.

Combine with the rest of the ingredients (except the garnish) in a high-speed blender with ½ cup crushed ice. Blend at high speed for 5 seconds.

Pour into a chilled cocktail glass and garnish with a mint sprig.

THREE DOTS AND A DASH

A cocktail created by Donn Beach to celebrate the end of World War Two, you're drinking a little bit of history with every sip of this one. Fun fact: The name translates to V (the sign of victory) in Morse code and is spelled out in the cherry and pineapple garnish.

SERVES 1

1 pineapple stick, for garnish

3 maraschino cherries, for garnish

1 oz (30 ml) rhum agricole (cane juice rum)

1 oz (30 ml) aged rum

1 oz (30 ml) lime juice

½ oz (15 ml) orange curaçao

½ oz (15 ml) Honey syrup (page 253)

½ oz (15 ml) Velvet falernum (page 257)

¼ oz (7.5 ml) Allspice dram (page 259)

3 dashes Orange bitters (page 258)

To make the garnish, thread the pineapple stick and three cherries onto a skewer.

Place the ingredients (except the garnish) in a high-speed blender with ½ cup crushed ice. Blend at high speed for 5 seconds.

Pour into a highball glass and top with crushed ice. Place the skewer across the top, ensuring that it's facing the right way so it reads as three dots and a dash.

MISSIONARY'S DOWNFALL

One of Donn Beach's early recipes, this tiki mainstay can be traced back to the late 1930s. Packing a cocktail with fresh mint might seem like standard practice these days, but Donn himself pioneered the use of herbs in cocktails. When you sip one of these, you're imbibing tiki heritage.

SERVES 1

2 oz (60 ml) white rum
½ oz (15 ml) peach liqueur
1½ oz (¼ cup) diced pineapple
1½ oz (45 ml) freshly squeezed lime juice
½ oz (15 ml) Sugar syrup (page 250)
1 small handful mint, chopped, for garnish

Place the ingredients (except the garnish) in a high-speed blender with 1 cup ice and blend at high speed until smooth.

Pour into a chilled cocktail glass. Garnish with mint.

SHARK'S TOOTH

A boilermaker brew to enjoy with a side of your best aged rum, this might just be the only shark's tooth you'll be happy to be touched by while you're on vacation.

SERVES 1

1 oz (30 ml) good-quality aged rum
1 oz (30 ml) gold rum
½ oz (15 ml) freshly squeezed lime juice
½ oz (15 ml) pineapple juice, fresh if possible
½ oz (15 ml) Sugar syrup (page 250)
⅙ oz (5 ml) maraschino cherry liqueur (or juice)
maraschino cherry, for garnish

Pour the aged rum into a shot glass or tumbler.

Place the remaining ingredients (except the garnish) in a high-speed blender with ½ cup crushed ice. Blend at high speed for 5 seconds.

Strain into a cocktail glass filled with crushed ice. Garnish with a maraschino cherry with the aged rum on the side.

PI YI

It's a truth universally acknowledged that drinking a cocktail from a hollowed-out pineapple just hits different. Go on, take the plunge and be at one with the pineapple vessel. One sip and you'll forget all about the existence of cocktail glasses anyway.

SERVES 1

1 oz (30 ml) white rum
1 oz (30 ml) gold rum
1½ oz (45 ml) pineapple juice, fresh if possible
½ oz (15 ml) Honey syrup (page 253)
½ oz (15 ml) Passionfruit syrup (page 256)
1 dash Orange bitters (page 258)
hollowed pineapple, for serving (optional)
pineapple leaves and maraschino cherries, for garnish

Place the rums, pineapple juice, syrups and bitters in a high-speed blender with ½ cup crushed ice. Blend at high speed for 5 seconds.

Pour into a hollowed-out pineapple (or large cocktail glass) and top with crushed ice.

Garnish with pineapple leaves and maraschino cherries.

MONTEGO BAY

*With three different types of rum,
a dash of absinthe and a shot of spice,
there's a lot going on in this big,
boozy cocktail. Sit with this one
a while to truly appreciate
the depth of flavor.*

SERVES 1

⅔ oz (20 ml) dark rum

⅔ oz (20 ml) gold rum

⅔ oz (20 ml) aged rum

⅙ oz (5 ml) absinthe

½ oz (15 ml) freshly squeezed lime juice

½ oz (15 ml) freshly squeezed grapefruit juice

⅔ oz (20 ml) Honey syrup (page 253)

⅙ oz (5 ml) Allspice dram (page 259)

1 dash Orange bitters (page 258)

grapefruit wheel, for garnish

Combine the ingredients (except the garnish) in
a cocktail shaker filled with ice. Shake.

Strain into a chilled cocktail glass filled with crushed
ice. Garnish with a grapefruit wheel.

SUMATRA KULA

Another Donn Beach recipe from the early tiki era, this cooler is remarkable in that it's sweetened with honey syrup instead of pineapple or sugar. The result is a sweet and simple cocktail that's effortless to drink.

SERVES 1

1½ oz (45 ml) aged rum

1 oz (30 ml) rhum agricole (cane juice rum)

½ oz (15 ml) freshly squeezed grapefruit juice

½ oz (15 ml) freshly squeezed lime juice

½ oz (15 ml) freshly squeezed orange juice

½ oz (15 ml) Honey syrup (page 253)

mint sprig and lime wheel, orange wheel or grapefruit wheel (or a combination), for garnish

Combine the ingredients (except the garnish) in a cocktail shaker filled with crushed ice and shake.

Pour the contents of the shaker into a highball glass and top with crushed ice. Garnish with mint and your choice of citrus wheels.

SHONKY DONKEY

A Moscow Mule made with rum, this slightly spicy muddled cocktail is one for fans of the winning combination that is ginger, mint and lime.

SERVES 1

1 lime, cut into 8 wedges
1 small handful mint leaves
⅓ oz (10 ml) Sugar syrup (page 250)
2 oz (60 ml) spiced rum
3½ oz (105 ml) ginger beer
mint sprig and lime wedge, for garnish

Muddle the lime and mint leaves in a cocktail shaker. Add the sugar syrup, rum and 1 cup ice. Shake vigorously.

Pour the contents of the shaker into a copper mug or highball glass and add more ice if needed. Top up with ginger beer.

Garnish with mint and a lime wedge.

COBRA'S FANG

One from Don the Beachcomber's cocktail list, as the name suggests this is a cocktail not to be messed with thanks to the inclusion of absinthe and 151 proof rum. Sssssssssip this one slowly!

SERVES 1

½ oz (15 ml) dark rum
1 oz (30 ml) 151 proof rum
⅓ oz (10 ml) absinthe
½ oz (15 ml) freshly squeezed lime juice
½ oz (15 ml) freshly squeezed orange juice
½ oz (15 ml) Velvet falernum (page 257)
½ oz (15 ml) Grenadine (page 251)
1 dash Orange bitters (page 258)
cinnamon stick, for garnish

Place the ingredients (except the garnish) in a high-speed blender with ½ cup crushed ice. Blend at high speed for 5 seconds.

Pour into an old fashioned glass and top with crushed ice. Garnish with a cinnamon stick.

MOONKIST COCONUT

What's better than drinking alcohol out of a coconut? Doing it while you're suspended in the air between two trees. If you're in the mood, tack on one more step to this recipe: Just add hammock.

SERVES 1

1½ oz (45 ml) white rum

⅔ oz (20 ml) gold rum

¼ oz (7.5 ml) coconut rum

½ oz (15 ml) freshly squeezed lime juice

1 oz (30 ml) Rich honey syrup (page 253)

⅓ oz (10 ml) Velvet falernum (page 257)

1½ oz (45 ml) coconut milk

½ oz (15 ml) coconut cream

2 dashes Orange bitters (page 258)

opened coconut, for serving (optional)

pineapple leaves, for garnish

Place the ingredients (except the coconut and garnish) in a high-speed blender with 1 cup crushed ice. Blend at high speed for 5 seconds.

Pour into a coconut (or a large cocktail glass) and garnish with pineapple leaves.

SHRUNKEN SKULL

Use your head and put a novelty, skull-shaped tiki mug to good use with this suitably named, ghoulish cocktail that's perfect for Halloween parties.

SERVES 1

1 oz (30 ml) white rum
1 oz (30 ml) demerara rum
1 oz (30 ml) Grenadine (page 251)
1 oz (30 ml) freshly squeezed lime juice
pomegranate seeds, for garnish

Combine the ingredients (except the garnish) in a cocktail shaker filled with ice. Shake.

Strain into a skull-shaped tiki mug or old fashioned glass filled with ice. Garnish with pomegranate seeds.

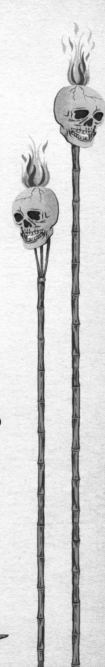

BLUE HAWAIIAN

Evoke the spirit of the 1960s with this retro classic that's the closest thing you'll get to a Waikiki resort bar drink, without getting on a plane to Hawaii.

SERVES 1

1 oz (30 ml) white rum
1 oz (30 ml) vodka
½ oz (15 ml) blue curaçao
3 oz (90 ml) pineapple juice, fresh if possible
1 oz (30 ml) freshly squeezed lime juice
½ oz (15 ml) Sugar syrup (page 250)
pineapple wedge, maraschino cherry and cocktail umbrella, for garnish

Combine the ingredients (except the garnish) in a cocktail shaker filled with ice. Shake.

Strain into a highball glass filled with ice and garnish with a pineapple wedge, maraschino cherry and cocktail umbrella.

BEACHCOMBER'S PUNCH

Since Donn Beach created this recipe in the early days of tiki, it's best to salute this heritage drink with a suitably retro garnish. This is the mini cocktail umbrella's time to shine.

SERVES 1

2 oz (60 ml) demerara rum
½ oz (15 ml) apricot brandy
⅙ oz (5 ml) Pernod
½ oz (15 ml) freshly squeezed lime juice
½ oz (15 ml) freshly squeezed grapefruit juice
½ oz (15 ml) Sugar syrup (page 250)
1 dash Orange bitters (page 258)
mint sprig and cocktail umbrella, for garnish

Place the ingredients (except the garnish) in a high-speed blender with crushed ice. Blend at high speed for 5 seconds.

Pour into a chilled highball glass and top up with more crushed ice if necessary. Garnish with mint and a cocktail umbrella.

MOJITO

One of Cuba's greatest exports, the mighty Mojito has taken the world by storm. Learn how to make a mean Mojito and you'll never be short of company.

SERVES 1

½ lime, cut into 6 pieces
1 small handful mint leaves
½ oz (15 g) sugar
2 oz (60 ml) dark Cuban rum
1½ oz (45 ml) soda water
mint sprig and lime wedge, for garnish

Muddle the lime, mint leaves and sugar in a cocktail shaker. Add the rum and fill the shaker with ice. Shake vigorously.

Pour the contents of the shaker into a highball glass and top with the soda water. Garnish with mint and a lime wedge.

PINEAPPLE MOJITO

Reinvent the Mojito by adding some pineapple and swapping the mint for basil. Add a hammock to the equation and now you're talking.

SERVES 1

1 lime, cut into 12 pieces
5½ oz (1 cup) chopped fresh pineapple
1 small handful basil leaves
3 oz (90 ml) white rum
1 oz (30 ml) Sugar syrup (page 250)
2 oz (60 ml) soda water
hollowed-out pineapple, for serving (optional)
lemongrass stalk, for garnish

Muddle the lime, chopped pineapple and basil in a cocktail shaker. Add the rum and sugar syrup and fill the shaker with crushed ice. Shake vigorously.

Pour the contents of the shaker into a hollowed-out pineapple (or a very large glass) and top up with crushed ice and the soda water. Garnish with lemongrass and two straws.

BLUEBERRY MOJITO

Packed with antioxidant-rich blueberries, you could almost convince yourself that this style of Mojito is actually good for you.

SERVES 1

1 lime, cut into 12 pieces

5½ oz (1 cup) fresh blueberries, plus extra for garnish

1 small handful mint leaves

1½ oz (45 ml) white rum

1 oz (30 ml) umeshu (Japanese plum wine)

1 oz (30 ml) Sugar syrup (page 250)

2 oz (60 ml) soda water

lime wedge, for garnish

Muddle the lime, blueberries and mint in a cocktail shaker. Add the rum, umeshu and sugar syrup. Fill the shaker with ice and shake vigorously.

Pour the contents of the shaker into a highball glass and top up with ice. Add the soda water. Garnish with blueberries and a lime wedge.

FREMANTLE DOCTOR

Named after an Australian slang term for a cool afternoon breeze that arrives off the coast of Perth, this cocktail is as refreshing on a hot day as its namesake.

SERVES 1

1 oz (30 ml) white rum
½ oz (15 ml) apricot brandy
1 oz (30 ml) freshly squeezed lemon juice
3 oz (90 ml) pineapple juice, fresh if possible
½ oz (15 ml) Galliano
blood orange wheel and maraschino cherry,
for garnish

Combine the rum, brandy and fruit juices in a cocktail shaker filled with ice. Shake.

Strain into a highball glass filled with ice. Float the Galliano on top by pouring it over the back of a spoon.

Garnish with a blood orange wheel and a maraschino cherry.

BEHIND THE BIKE SHED

*A cheeky tipple you won't need
to hide your passion for. Feel free to
enjoy one of these out in the open.*

SERVES 1

2 oz (60 ml) white rum

2 oz (60 ml) gold rum

2 oz (60 ml) freshly squeezed pink grapefruit juice

3 oz (90 ml) pineapple juice, fresh if possible

½ oz (15 ml) Passionfruit syrup (page 256)

2 oz (60 ml) lemonade

⅙ oz (5 ml) maraschino cherry liqueur (or juice)

maraschino cherries and lime wheels, for garnish

Combine the rums, fruit juices and passionfruit
syrup in a cocktail shaker filled with ice. Shake.

Strain into two highball glasses filled with ice. Top
with the lemonade and maraschino liqueur.

Garnish with maraschino cherries and lime wheels.

RUM 'N' RASPBERRIES

Sure, its name might be a tad unimaginative, but when the flavor combination of rum and raspberries is this good, a clever cocktail name isn't needed to sell it.

SERVES 1

2 oz (½ cup) fresh raspberries, plus extra for garnish
1½ oz (45 ml) spiced rum
½ oz (15 ml) raspberry liqueur
½ oz (15 ml) lime juice
1 dash Orange bitters (page 258)
⅓ oz (10 ml) agave syrup

Muddle the raspberries in a cocktail shaker. Add the remaining ingredients (except the garnish) along with ½ cup ice. Shake vigorously.

Pour the contents of the shaker into an old fashioned glass and top with ice if necessary. Garnish with fresh raspberries.

BIG BAMBOO
LOVE SONG

A liquid love song dedicated to the zesty wonder of citrus, the lemongrass stalk merges form and function as both a tasty garnish and biodegradable swizzle stick.

SERVES 1

2 oz (60 ml) dark rum
1 oz (30 ml) white rum
½ oz (15 ml) orange curaçao
1 oz (30 ml) freshly squeezed orange juice
2 oz (60 ml) pineapple juice, fresh if possible
1 oz (30 ml) freshly squeezed lime juice
bruised lemongrass stalk, for garnish

Combine the ingredients (except the garnish) in a cocktail shaker filled with ice. Shake.

Strain into a highball glass filled with crushed ice. Garnish with a bruised lemongrass stalk.

JAMAICAN ME CRAZY

You'll go troppo for this blended cocktail packed with Jamaican rum, coconut rum and banana liqueur.

SERVES 1

1 oz (30 ml) Jamaican rum
1 oz (30 ml) coconut rum
½ oz (15 ml) banana liqueur
⅓ oz (10 ml) Grenadine (page 251)
1 oz (30 ml) pineapple juice, fresh if possible
1 oz (30 ml) cranberry juice
lime wheel, for garnish

Place the ingredients (except the garnish) in a high-speed blender with 1 cup ice and blend at high speed until smooth.

Pour into a hurricane glass and garnish with a lime wheel.

BLUE MULLET

Named after a fish that's known to leap out of the water, you too will find some get-up-and-go after downing one of these ice-cold cocktails.

SERVES 1

1½ oz (45 ml) white rum
½ oz (15 ml) coconut rum
⅓ oz (10 ml) blue curaçao
⅓ oz (10 ml) freshly squeezed lime juice
⅓ oz (10 ml) freshly squeezed lemon juice
⅓ oz (10 ml) Sugar syrup (page 250)
1 oz (30 ml) freshly squeezed orange juice
maraschino cherry, for garnish

Combine the ingredients (except the garnish) in a cocktail shaker filled with ice. Shake.

Strain into an old fashioned glass filled with ice. Garnish with a maraschino cherry.

CARIBBEAN SUNSET

What's better than witnessing a glorious, golden sunset? Doing it with this smooth cocktail in your hand.

SERVES 1

1½ oz (45 ml) white rum
½ oz (15 ml) coconut rum
2 oz (60 ml) pineapple juice, fresh if possible
2 oz (60 ml) freshly squeezed orange juice
½ oz (15 ml) Grenadine (page 251)
pineapple wedge, for garnish

Combine the rums and fruit juices in a cocktail shaker filled with ice. Shake.

Strain into a highball glass filled with ice. Add the grenadine and garnish with a pineapple wedge.

CARIBBEAN ISLAND ICED COFFEE

*Introducing the caffeinated cousin
of the Long Island Iced Tea, this refreshing
coffee cocktail will put a spring
in your step.*

SERVES 1

1 oz (30 ml) Jamaican rum
1 oz (30 ml) white rum
½ oz (15 ml) coffee liqueur
⅔ oz (20 ml) sweetened condensed milk
3 oz (90 ml) espresso, chilled
coffee beans, for garnish

Combine the ingredients (except the garnish) in
a cocktail shaker filled with ice. Shake.

Strain into a highball glass filled with ice. Garnish
with coffee beans.

RUM DADDY

*The big daddy of rums,
aged rum is the main ingredient
in this citrus cocktail best suited
to mature drinkers.*

SERVES 1

2 oz (60 ml) aged rum
½ oz (15 ml) Pernod
½ oz (15 ml) Velvet falernum (page 257)
1 oz (30 ml) Sugar syrup (page 250)
1 oz (30 ml) freshly squeezed lime juice
2 dashes Orange bitters (page 258)
orange wheel, for garnish

Combine the ingredients (except the garnish) in
a cocktail shaker filled with ice. Shake.

Strain into a highball glass filled with crushed ice.
Garnish with an orange wheel.

MENEHUNE JUICE

In Hawaiian folklore, encountering an elf-like menehune is said to bring good fortune. Try enhancing your luck by drinking a few of these.

SERVES 1

2 oz (60 ml) white rum

½ oz (15 ml) orange curaçao

⅓ oz (10 ml) Orgeat syrup (page 252)

⅓ oz (10 ml) Sugar syrup (page 250)

1 oz (30 ml) freshly squeezed lime juice

mint sprig and lime wheel, for garnish

Combine the ingredients (except the garnish) in a cocktail shaker filled with crushed ice. Shake.

Strain into a highball glass and top with crushed ice. Garnish with mint and a lime wheel.

KONA GOLD

Not to be confused with the brand of coffee with the same name, this cherry-infused cocktail is a caffeine-free affair, so is safe to sip after dark.

SERVES 1

2 oz (60 ml) gold rum
⅙ oz (5 ml) maraschino cherry liqueur (or juice)
1 oz (30 ml) Don's mix (page 261)
½ oz (15 ml) Pernod
maraschino cherry, for garnish

Combine the rum, cherry liqueur and Don's mix in a cocktail shaker filled with ice. Shake.

Strain into an old fashioned glass filled with crushed ice. Float the Pernod on top by pouring it over the back of a spoon.

Garnish with a maraschino cherry.

LAPU LAPU

*A city in the Philippines
and a celebrated Filipino hero
are two things that go by the name
"Lapu Lapu." The third is this
strong cocktail laced with
151 proof rum.*

SERVES 1

2 oz (60 ml) dark rum
1 oz (30 ml) pineapple juice, fresh if possible
2 oz (60 ml) freshly squeezed orange juice
½ oz (15 ml) freshly squeezed lime juice
½ oz (15 ml) freshly squeezed lemon juice
½ oz (15 ml) Sugar syrup (page 250)
½ oz (15 ml) 151 proof rum
pineapple wedge, lemon wheel and lime twist,
for garnish

Combine the dark rum, fruit juices and sugar
syrup in a cocktail shaker filled with ice. Shake.

Strain into a highball glass filled with ice. Float the
151 proof rum on top by pouring it over the back
of a spoon.

Garnish with a pineapple wedge, lemon wheel and
lime twist and drink through a straw.

POMME AND CINNAMONY

If you love warm apple pie, then try this cold version (sans pastry) that shows why apple and cinnamon are such great bedfellows.

SERVES 1

1 oz (30 ml) white rum
1 oz (30 ml) gold rum
½ oz (15 ml) freshly squeezed lime juice
½ oz (15 ml) Cinnamon syrup (page 255)
2 oz (60 ml) cloudy apple juice
apple slices and ground cinnamon,
for garnish

Combine the ingredients (except the garnish)
in a cocktail shaker filled with ice. Shake.

Strain into a highball glass filled with ice.
Garnish with apple slices and a dusting
of cinnamon.

VIRGIN SACRIFICE

Thankfully, when drinking this cocktail the only thing you'll have to sacrifice is your sobriety.

SERVES 1

2 oz (60 ml) gold rum

½ oz (15 ml) coconut rum

3 oz (90 ml) guava juice

1 oz (30 ml) pineapple juice, fresh if possible

½ oz (15 ml) freshly squeezed lime juice

⅓ oz (10 ml) Sugar syrup (page 250)

maraschino cherry, for garnish

Combine the ingredients (except the garnish) in a cocktail shaker filled with ice. Shake.

Strain into a highball glass filled with crushed ice. Garnish with a maraschino cherry.

GLASS SLIPPER

Containing a potent mix of sugar cane rum and super-strong 151 proof rum, to avoid a hangover drink this one before the clock strikes 12, not after.

SERVES 1

2 oz (60 ml) rhum agricole (sugar cane rum)
⅔ oz (20 ml) elderflower liqueur
⅔ oz (20 ml) lemon juice
½ oz (15 ml) Vanilla syrup (page 254)
⅓ oz (10 ml) 151 proof rum
edible flowers, for garnish

Combine the rhum agricole, elderflower liqueur, lemon juice and vanilla syrup in a cocktail shaker filled with ice. Shake.

Strain into an old fashioned glass filled with crushed ice. Float the 151 proof rum on top by pouring it over the back of a spoon. Garnish with edible flowers.

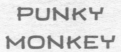

PUNKY MONKEY

Spice up your life with this cheeky tipple that lingers on the palate thanks to the tag team of cardamom and star anise.

SERVES 1

3 cardamom pods
1 oz (30 ml) aged rum
1 oz (30 ml) bourbon
½ oz (15 ml) agave nectar
½ oz (15 ml) pineapple juice, fresh if possible
½ oz (15 ml) freshly squeezed lemon juice
1 dash Orange bitters (page 258)
star anise, for garnish

Muddle the cardamom pods in a cocktail shaker. Add the remaining ingredients (except the garnish) and fill the shaker with ice. Shake vigorously.

Strain into a chilled cocktail glass and garnish with star anise.

POTTED PARROT

*Need an afternoon
pick-me-up? Perch yourself
on a bar stool, make friends
with this nutty cocktail and
you'll soon take flight.*

SERVES 1

2 oz (60 ml) white rum
½ oz (15 ml) orange curaçao
2 oz (60 ml) freshly squeezed orange juice
1 oz (30 ml) freshly squeezed lemon juice
⅓ oz (10 ml) Orgeat syrup (page 252)
⅓ oz (10 ml) Sugar syrup (page 250)
mint sprig, for garnish

Combine the ingredients (except the garnish) in
a cocktail shaker filled with ice. Shake.

Strain into an old fashioned glass filled with ice.
Garnish with mint.

QUEEN'S PARK SWIZZLE

Created back in the 1920s at the Queen's Park Hotel in Trinidad, this simple yet satisfying swizzle is a bit like a Mojito reimagined.

SERVES 1

½ oz (15 ml) freshly squeezed lime juice

2 mint sprigs, plus extra for garnish

2 oz (60 ml) dark rum

2 dashes Orange bitters (page 258)

½ oz (15 ml) Sugar syrup (page 250)

2 oz (60 ml) soda water

Place the lime juice and mint in a swizzle cup. Fill with crushed ice.

Add the rum, bitters and sugar syrup. Stir to combine and top with soda. Garnish with mint.

MARTINIQUE SWIZZLE

A vehicle for showcasing the rich, deep flavors of high-quality Martinque rum, this bittersweet swizzle is best savored somewhere warm and sunny.

SERVES 1

2 oz (60 ml) Martinique gold rum
⅓ oz (10 ml) Pernod
½ oz (15 ml) freshly squeezed lime juice
⅓ oz (10 ml) Sugar syrup (page 250)
2 dashes Orange bitters (page 258)
mint sprig and lime wheel, for garnish

Combine the ingredients (except the garnish) in a highball glass filled with crushed ice and stir to combine.

Garnish with mint and a lime wheel.

MOLOKAI MIKE

*For fans of aesthetically
pleasing cocktails, this showy
Trader Vic's creation is best served
in a fancy glass to showcase
its colorful layers.*

SERVES 1

1 oz (30 ml) white rum
½ oz (15 ml) brandy
1 oz (30 ml) freshly squeezed orange juice
1 oz (30 ml) freshly squeezed lemon juice
½ oz (15 ml) Orgeat syrup (page 252)
½ oz (15 ml) dark rum
⅓ oz (10 ml) Grenadine (page 251)
orange wheel and lemon wheel, for garnish

Combine the white rum, brandy, fruit juices
and orgeat syrup in a cocktail shaker filled
with ice. Shake.

Strain into a fancy-looking glass half-filled
with crushed ice.

Combine the dark rum and grenadine in a cocktail
shaker with ½ cup crushed ice and shake.

Gently pour into the glass to layer. Garnish with
an orange wheel and a lemon wheel.

RUMBLE IN THE JUNGLE

*If you like your cocktails long
and strong then you'll be delighted
with this potent potion.
Featuring four different
types of rum, hold back on
drinking too many of
these, lest you end
up punch drunk.*

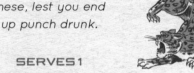

SERVES 1

1 oz (30 ml) spiced rum
½ oz (15 ml) coconut rum
½ oz (15 ml) dark rum
½ oz (15 ml) white rum
2 oz (60 ml) freshly squeezed orange juice
2 oz (60 ml) pineapple juice, fresh if possible
½ oz (15 ml) Grenadine (page 251)
pineapple wedge and orange wheel, for garnish

Place the ingredients (except the garnish) in
a high-speed blender with 1 cup crushed ice.
Blend at high speed for 5 seconds.

Pour into a highball glass and garnish with
a pineapple wedge and orange wheel.

FLYING DUTCHMAN

Named after the ghost ship forever doomed to sail the seven seas communicating only with the dead, thankfully this cocktail isn't an apparition.

SERVES 1

1 oz (30 ml) dark rum

1 oz (30 ml) rhum agricole (cane juice rum)

1½ oz (45 ml) cranberry juice

½ oz (15 ml) pineapple juice, fresh if possible

⅓ oz (10 ml) Grenadine (page 251)

2 dashes Orange bitters (page 258)

mint sprig, for garnish

Combine the ingredients (except the garnish) in a cocktail shaker filled with ice. Shake.

Strain into a highball glass filled with ice. Garnish with mint.

LUCY LOU

*Creamy cocktail lovers will
delight in this banana, rum, sherry
and cream liqueur-infused number. Served
in a voluptuous glass and garnished with
delicate flowers, this cocktail with
feminine energy can be appreciated
by all genders.*

SERVES 1

1 oz (30 ml) aged rum
1½ oz (45 ml) cream liqueur
½ oz (15 ml) oloroso sherry
¼ banana
½ oz (15 ml) Sugar syrup (page 250)
pinch of salt
tropical flower and vanilla beans, for garnish

Place the ingredients (except the garnish) in
a high-speed blender with 1 cup crushed ice.
Blend at high speed for 5 seconds.

Pour into a poco grande glass. Garnish with
a tropical flower and vanilla beans.

HUKILAU

*Named after a traditional
Hawaiian style of catching fish,
you don't need to be good
at fishing to enjoy this tantalizing
tipple that gets its tang from
spiced rum, ginger liqueur
and a dash of lime.*

SERVES 1

1 oz (30 ml) spiced rum
½ oz (15 ml) ginger liqueur
⅓ oz (10 ml) amaretto
2 oz (60 ml) pineapple juice, fresh if possible
1 oz (30 ml) freshly squeezed orange juice
½ oz (15 ml) freshly squeezed lime juice
orange wheel and lime wedge, for garnish

Combine the ingredients (except the garnish) in
a cocktail shaker filled with ice. Shake.

Strain into an old fashioned glass filled with ice.
Garnish with an orange wheel and a lime wedge.

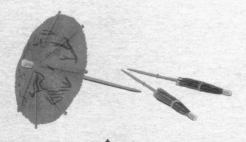

SIBONEY

*Sharing a name with a classic
Cuban tune about yearning for
something you can't have, you'll also be
longing for another one of these cocktails.
One just never seems enough.*

SERVES 1

1 oz (30 ml) dark rum
1 oz (30 ml) white rum
½ oz (15 ml) lemon juice
½ oz (15 ml) Passionfruit syrup (page 256)
½ oz (15 ml) pineapple juice, fresh if possible
pineapple wedge and maraschino cherry,
for garnish

Combine the ingredients (except the garnish) in
a cocktail shaker filled with ice. Shake.

Strain into a chilled cocktail glass. Garnish with
a pineapple wedge and maraschino cherry.

TABU

A citrusy, blended cocktail heavy on cane juice rum and mint, this spiked slushy is strictly an adults-only affair.

SERVES 1

2 oz (60 ml) rhum agricole (cane juice rum)
3 oz (90 ml) pineapple juice, fresh if possible
1 oz (30 ml) cranberry juice
½ oz (15 ml) Sugar syrup (page 250)
½ oz (15 ml) freshly squeezed lemon juice
6 mint leaves
mint sprig, for garnish

Place the ingredients (except the garnish) in a high-speed blender with 1 cup ice. Blend at high speed until smooth.

Pour into a hurricane glass and garnish with mint.

TAHITIAN GOLD

Having trouble relaxing?
Whip up one of these rum and
lime concoctions and you'll be
good as gold in no time.

SERVES 1

2 oz (60 ml) gold rum
⅙ oz (5 ml) maraschino cherry liqueur (or juice)
1 oz (30 ml) freshly squeezed lime juice
½ oz (15 ml) Sugar syrup (page 250)
⅙ oz (5 ml) Pernod

Combine the ingredients (except the Pernod) in
a cocktail shaker filled with ice. Shake.

Strain into a chilled cocktail glass and float
the Pernod on top by pouring it over the back
of a spoon.

BARREL O' RUM

If you've got some highly flammable 151 proof rum
gathering dust in your cocktail cabinet, then fire up
your next party with this retro-tastic tipple.

SERVES 1

2 oz (60 ml) white rum

2 oz (60 ml) dark rum

2 oz (60 ml) freshly squeezed lime juice

2 oz (60 ml) freshly squeezed orange juice

2 oz (60 ml) freshly squeezed grapefruit juice

2 oz (60 ml) Passionfruit syrup (page 256)

⅙ oz (5 ml) Rich honey syrup (page 253)

½ oz (15 ml) soda water

⅙ oz (5 ml) Orange bitters (page 258)

½ passionfruit

⅓ oz (10 ml) 151 proof rum

Place the white and dark rum, fruit juices, syrups, soda water
and bitters in a high-speed blender with 1 cup crushed ice.
Blend at high speed for 5 seconds.

Pour into a ceramic rum barrel mug or large brandy balloon.
Top with the half passionfruit. Pour the 151 proof rum into the
passionfruit and carefully ignite. After 15 seconds, blow out the
flame and tip the rum into the drink.

FOG CUTTER

A tiki classic with disputed origins, you'll definitely want to drink this one with a straw to ensure the rich hit of amontillado sherry arrives at just the right time.

SERVES 1

2 oz (60 ml) white rum

1 oz (30 ml) brandy or cognac

½ oz (15 ml) dry gin

2 oz (60 ml) freshly squeezed lemon juice

1 oz (30 ml) freshly squeezed orange juice

½ oz (15 ml) Orgeat syrup (page 252)

½ oz (15 ml) amontillado sherry

orange wheel and maraschino cherry, for garnish

Combine the rum, brandy or cognac, gin, fruit juices and orgeat syrup in a cocktail shaker filled with ice. Shake.

Strain into a highball glass filled with ice. Float the sherry on top by pouring it over the back of a spoon. Garnish with an orange wheel and a maraschino cherry.

FULL MOON PARTY

Take a walk on the wild side and whip up this heady cocktail containing once-illicit absinthe. Take it to the next level by imbibing on a full moon, if you dare.

SERVES 1

2 oz (60 ml) dark rum
½ oz (15 ml) absinthe
2 oz (60 ml) freshly squeezed lime juice
½ oz (15 ml) freshly squeezed lemon juice
½ oz (15 ml) Grenadine (page 251)
3 oz (90 ml) soda water
lime wheel, for garnish

Combine the ingredients (except the soda water and garnish) in a cocktail shaker filled with ice. Shake.

Strain into a highball glass filled with crushed ice. Top with the soda water and garnish with a lime wheel.

THE CASTAWAY

The mellowness of gold rum mixed with the earthy, nuttiness of amaretto is an intoxicating combination that's so good, you'll be tempted to take your cocktail to a deserted island to enjoy it all to yourself.

SERVES 1

1 oz (30 ml) gold rum

1 oz (30 ml) amaretto

2 oz (60 ml) pineapple juice, fresh if possible

½ oz (15 ml) freshly squeezed lime juice

⅓ oz (10 ml) coconut cream

⅓ oz (10 ml) Sugar syrup (page 250)

2 dashes Orange bitters (page 258)

maraschino cherries, for garnish

Combine the ingredients (except the garnish) in a cocktail shaker filled with ice. Shake.

Strain into a highball glass filled with ice. Garnish with maraschino cherries.

BEACHCOMBER'S GOLD

*Another cocktail made famous at
Don the Beachcomber, one sip of this rum
and vermouth tipple and you'll think
you've struck gold.*

SERVES 1

1 oz (30 ml) aged rum
1 oz (30 ml) white rum
½ oz (15 ml) sweet vermouth
½ oz (15 ml) dry vermouth
1 dash Orange bitters (page 258)
orange slice and maraschino cherry, for garnish

Combine the ingredients (except the garnish) in a
cocktail shaker filled with ice and stir vigorously.

Strain into a chilled cocktail glass. Garnish with an
orange slice and a maraschino cherry.

MARA AMU

A cocktail so influential it has its very own tiki glass, this drink was birthed at Fort Lauderdale's famous Mai-Kai restaurant but has since been replicated in tiki bars all over the world.

SERVES 1

½ oz (15 ml) white rum
½ oz (15 ml) gold rum
½ oz (15 ml) dark rum
⅔ oz (20 ml) freshly squeezed lime juice
⅔ oz (20 ml) freshly squeezed orange juice
⅔ oz (20 ml) freshly squeezed grapefruit juice
⅔ oz (20 ml) Passionfruit syrup (page 256)
pink grapefruit wedge, for garnish

Place the ingredients (except the garnish) in a high-speed blender with 1 cup crushed ice. Blend at high speed for 5 seconds.

Pour into a Mara Amu mug or highball glass. Garnish with a pink grapefruit wedge.

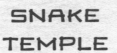

SNAKE TEMPLE

Made by infusing gin with sloe berries, sloe gin adds a little X-factor to this tantalizing tipple worthy of worship.

SERVES 1

1 oz (30 ml) gold rum
1 oz (30 ml) rhum agricole (cane juice rum)
½ oz (15 ml) sloe gin
⅔ oz (20 ml) freshly squeezed lime juice
½ oz (15 ml) Velvet falernum (page 257)
lime wheel, for garnish

Combine the ingredients (except the garnish) in a cocktail shaker filled with ice. Shake.

Strain into a highball glass filled with crushed ice. Garnish with a lime wheel.

TIKI
BOOM BOOM

*Impress your friends by whipping
up one of these visually impressive cocktails.
Carefully layer the multi-hued ingredient mixes
and – boom – you've got yourself a tri-color
cocktail that will dazzle your guests.*

SERVES 1

1 oz (30 ml) white rum
½ oz (15 ml) coconut rum
½ oz (15 ml) pineapple rum
2⅔ oz (80 ml) coconut water
½ oz (15 ml) freshly squeezed lemon juice
½ oz (15 ml) Sugar syrup (page 250)
⅓ oz (10 ml) Grenadine (page 251)
⅓ oz (10 ml) blue curaçao
maraschino cherry, for garnish

Combine the rums, coconut water, lemon juice and sugar
syrup in a cocktail shaker filled with ice and
shake vigorously.

Pour the grenadine into a poco grande glass and fill with
crushed ice. Strain the rum mixture slowly into the glass
and float the blue curaçao on top by pouring it over
the back of a spoon.

Garnish with a maraschino cherry.

EL PRESIDENTE

This Cuban concoction was first mixed more than century ago. After a long, post-Prohibition era hiatus, this classic was revisited by bartenders who put it back on the cocktail menu where it belongs.

SERVES 1

1½ oz (45 ml) white rum
1½ oz (45 ml) dry vermouth
⅙ oz (5 ml) orange curaçao
1/12 oz (2.5 ml) Grenadine (page 251)
orange twist and maraschino cherry, for garnish

Pour the ingredients (except the garnish) into a cocktail shaker filled with ice and stir vigorously.

Strain into a chilled cocktail glass.

Squeeze the orange twist over the drink to release the oils from the skin. Rub the rind along the rim of the glass. Drop the twist into the glass along with a maraschino cherry.

TORTUGA

Containing a liberal pour of overproof rum, this is a very stiff drink that will go to your head if you're not careful. You've been warned!

SERVES 1

1½ oz (45 ml) 151 proof rum
1 oz (30 ml) sweet vermouth
⅓ oz (10 ml) orange curaçao
1½ oz (45 ml) freshly squeezed orange juice
½ oz (15 ml) freshly squeezed lime juice
1 oz (30 ml) freshly squeezed lemon juice
⅓ oz (10 ml) Grenadine (page 251)
mint sprig and orange wheel, for garnish

Place the ingredients (except the garnish) in a high-speed blender filled with ice. Blend at high speed until smooth.

Pour into a double old fashioned glass and garnish with mint and an orange wheel.

RUM RUNNER

*Featuring an eclectic mix of rums, juices
and liqueurs, rumor has it that this tropical
treat was first created by a Florida bartender
who needed to use up left-over booze.
Whether this is true or not doesn't
matter; this is one delicious drink.*

SERVES 1

1 oz (30 ml) dark rum
1 oz (30 ml) white rum
1 oz (30 ml) blackberry liqueur
1 oz (30 ml) banana liqueur
1 oz (30 ml) freshly squeezed orange juice
1 oz (30 ml) pineapple juice, fresh if possible
⅓ oz (10 ml) Grenadine (page 251)
½ oz (15 ml) 151 proof white rum (optional)
orange slices and cocktail umbrella, for garnish

Place the dark and white rums, the liqueurs and the fruit juices
in a high-speed blender with 1 cup ice. Blend until smooth.

Pour into a hurricane glass and add the grenadine. If using,
float the 151 proof rum on top by pouring it over the back
of a spoon.

Garnish with orange slices and a cocktail umbrella.

JUNGLE BIRD

Transport yourself to another era with this refreshing tropical cocktail first created by a Malaysian bartender in the 1970s. The Campari really makes it sing...like a (jungle) bird.

SERVES 1

1½ oz (45 ml) gold rum
½ oz (15 ml) dark rum
⅔ oz (20 ml) Campari
1½ oz (45 ml) pineapple juice, fresh if possible
½ oz (15 ml) freshly squeezed lime juice
½ oz (15 ml) Sugar syrup (page 250)
orange wheel, for garnish

Combine the ingredients (except the garnish) in a cocktail shaker filled with ice. Shake.

Strain into an old fashioned glass filled with ice. Garnish with an orange wheel.

AKU AKU

Named after a benevolent spirit associated with Easter Island mythology, it's no mystery why this minty marvel is an enduring favorite with tiki cocktail lovers – it goes down a treat.

SERVES 1

1 oz (30 ml) white rum
½ oz (15 ml) peach liqueur
½ oz (15 ml) freshly squeezed lime juice
2 oz (⅓ cup) chopped pineapple
1 small handful mint leaves
½ oz (15 ml) Sugar syrup (page 250)
mint sprig and pineapple wedge, for garnish

Place the ingredients (except the garnish) in a high-speed blender with 1½ cups crushed ice. Blend until smooth.

Pour into an old fashioned glass and garnish with mint and a pineapple wedge.

ISLAND HOLIDAY

Can't afford a vacation to a tropical island? This thirst-quenching cocktail with a slight tang is the next best thing to a beach break.

SERVES 1

1 oz (30 ml) white rum
½ oz (15 ml) mango liqueur
½ oz (15 ml) melon liqueur
½ oz (15 ml) banana liqueur
2 oz (60 ml) freshly squeezed pink grapefruit juice
2 oz (60 ml) soda water
½ oz (15 ml) cranberry juice
pineapple wedge and leaves, for garnish

Pour the rum, liqueurs and grapefruit juice into a highball glass. Stir to combine.

Fill the glass with ice and top with soda and cranberry juice.

Garnish with a pineapple wedge and leaves.

ISLAND BREEZE

This fruity cocktail is as refreshing as a gentle sea breeze on a warm, sunny day.

SERVES 1

2 oz (60 ml) white rum

1 oz (30 ml) cranberry juice

3½ oz (105 ml) pineapple juice, fresh if possible

2 dashes Orange bitters (page 258)

maraschino cherry and lemon wheel,
for garnish

Combine the rum and cranberry juice in
a highball glass filled with ice.

Slowly add the pineapple juice, trying to leave
a blush of cranberry at the bottom. Add
the bitters.

Garnish with a maraschino cherry and
lemon wheel.

COCONUT KISS

Coconut fans will love locking lips with this creamy treat guaranteed to take the sting out of a hot day.

SERVES 1

1 oz (30 ml) coconut rum

1 oz (30 ml) white rum

⅔ oz (20 ml) cherry brandy

1 oz (30 ml) cream

⅓ oz (10 ml) Grenadine (page 251)

maraschino cherry and grated coconut, for garnish

Combine the ingredients (except the garnish) in a cocktail shaker filled with ice. Shake.

Strain into a chilled cocktail glass and garnish with a maraschino cherry and grated coconut.

148

SNEAKY TIKI

*Drink this one through a straw
and you'll soon see where this cocktail
gets its name. The closer you get
toward the bottom, the more
alcohol you'll taste.*

SERVES 1

2 oz (60 ml) white rum
½ oz (15 ml) blue curaçao
1 oz (30 ml) mango juice
1 oz (30 ml) guava juice
½ oz (15 ml) pineapple juice, fresh if possible
½ oz (15 ml) freshly squeezed lime juice
½ oz (15 ml) aged rum
lime wheel, for garnish

Combine the white rum, blue curaçao and fruit
juices in a cocktail shaker filled with ice. Shake.

Strain into a hurricane glass filled with ice. Float
the aged rum on top by pouring it over the
back of a spoon. Garnish with a lime wheel.

OUTRIGGER

A citrusy cocktail that's perfect for drinkers who prefer their tipples on the slightly sour side. One sip and you'll be sailing with the wind.

SERVES 1

1 oz (30 ml) white rum
1 oz (30 ml) gold rum
¼ oz (7.5 ml) orange curaçao
¼ oz (7.5 ml) Grenadine (page 251)
1 oz (30 ml) freshly squeezed orange juice
1 oz (30 ml) freshly squeezed lemon juice
pineapple wedge, for garnish

Combine the ingredients (except the garnish) in a cocktail shaker filled with ice. Shake.

Strain into a chilled cocktail glass. Garnish with a pineapple wedge.

FIRECRACKER

This chili-infused cocktail is guaranteed to make your tiki party go off with a bang (no pyrotechnics required).

SERVES 1

1 lime, cut into 8 pieces
3 oz (½ cup) chopped fresh watermelon
2 oz (60 ml) aged rum
1 oz (30 ml) orange curaçao
1 oz (30 ml) Sugar syrup (page 250)
1 pinch chili powder
watermelon wedge and sliced chili, for garnish

Muddle the lime and watermelon in a cocktail shaker. Add the rum, curaçao, sugar syrup and chili powder. Fill the shaker with ice and shake vigorously.

Strain into an old fashioned glass filled with ice. Garnish with a watermelon wedge and sliced chili.

151 SWIZZLE

You'll pick up rich caramel and molasses notes from the 151 proof demerara rum featured in this icy swizzle. Too strong? Letting the ice melt a little will take the edge off.

SERVES 1

1½ oz (45 ml) 151 proof demerara rum
½ oz (15 ml) freshly squeezed lime juice
½ oz (15 ml) Don's mix (page 261)
1 dash Orange bitters (page 258)
⅙ oz (5 ml) Pernod
cinnamon stick, lime wheel and freshly grated nutmeg, for garnish

Place the ingredients (except the garnish) in a high-speed blender with 1 cup crushed ice. Blend at high speed for 5 seconds.

Pour into a chilled swizzle or other stainless steel cup and top up with ice. Garnish with a cinnamon stick, lime wheel and grated nutmeg.

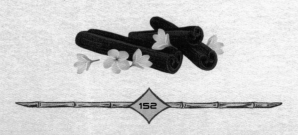

VANILLA GORILLA

Nothing says tropical cocktail more than an ingredient combination like rum, vanilla, banana and lime. Your guests will go ape for this one.

SERVES 1

1 oz (30 ml) white rum
1 oz (30 ml) aged rum
½ oz (15 ml) Licor 43
⅓ oz (10 ml) banana liqueur
⅔ oz (20 ml) freshly squeezed lime juice
¼ teaspoon vanilla extract
vanilla bean, for garnish

Combine the ingredients (except the garnish) in a cocktail shaker filled with ice. Shake.

Strain into an old fashioned glass filled with crushed ice. Garnish with a vanilla bean.

GOLDEN COLADA

Give the classic Piña Colada an upgrade by tinkering with a few ingredients. The addition of Galliano is a real gamechanger.

SERVES 1

1½ oz (45 ml) dark rum
1 oz (30 ml) gold rum
⅓ oz (10 ml) Galliano
½ oz (15 ml) coconut cream
1⅓ oz (40 ml) freshly squeezed orange juice
1 oz (30 ml) pineapple juice, fresh if possible
pineapple wedge, for garnish

Place the ingredients (except the garnish) in a high-speed blender with 1 cup ice and blend at high speed until smooth.

Pour into a poco grande glass and garnish with a pineapple wedge.

BLACK MAGIC

Expand your cocktail repertoire beyond the basic Espresso Martini by dipping your toe into the dark arts. This brew is guaranteed to cast a spell on you.

SERVES 1

1½ oz (45 ml) dark rum
1½ oz (45 ml) aged rum
1½ oz (45 ml) freshly brewed espresso
⅔ oz (20 ml) freshly squeezed lime juice
⅔ oz (20 ml) freshly squeezed orange juice
⅔ oz (20 ml) freshly squeezed grapefruit juice
⅔ oz (20 ml) Rich honey syrup (page 253)
½ oz (15 ml) Don's mix (page 261)
1 dash Vanilla syrup (page 254)
1 dash Allspice dram (page 259)
2 dashes Orange bitters (page 258)
lemon twist, for garnish

Place the ingredients (except the garnish) in a high-speed blender with 1 cup crushed ice. Blend at high speed until frothy.

Pour into a large brandy balloon and garnish with a lemon twist.

VOODOO

Featuring three types of rum and a dash of smoky single malt whisky, this intoxicating cocktail is a quasi-religious experience.

SERVES 1

1 oz (30 ml) dark rum
1 oz (30 ml) aged rum
1 oz (30 ml) white rum
⅓ oz (10 ml) smoky single malt whisky
2 oz (60 ml) pineapple juice, fresh if possible
2 oz (60 ml) freshly squeezed orange juice
pineapple wedge and maraschino cherry,
for garnish

Place the ingredients (except the garnish) in a high-speed blender with 1 cup crushed ice. Blend at high speed for 5 seconds.

Pour into a highball glass and top with crushed ice. Garnish with a pineapple wedge and a maraschino cherry.

MUTINY

Party vibe fading fast?
Avoid a mutiny by whipping up
this caffeinated cocktail
that will surely set your
ship mates right again.

SERVES 1

1½ oz (45 ml) white rum

1½ oz (45 ml) dark rum

⅔ oz (20 ml) freshly squeezed orange juice

⅔ oz (20 ml) freshly squeezed lime juice

⅔ oz (20 ml) freshly squeezed grapefruit juice

½ oz (15 ml) Rich honey syrup (page 253)

½ oz (15 ml) Passionfruit syrup (page 256)

1½ oz (45 ml) freshly brewed espresso

⅓ oz (10 ml) Don's mix (page 261)

2 dashes Orange bitters (page 258)

⅙ oz (5 ml) Pernod

coffee beans, for garnish

Place the ingredients (except the garnish) in a
high-speed blender with 1 cup crushed ice and
blend at high speed until frothy.

Pour into a large brandy balloon. Garnish
with coffee beans.

While rum plays a starring role in the land of tiki, there are plenty of other spirits to play with. Vodka, gin, tequila, whiskey, brandy, bourbon and beyond can all be given the tiki treatment if you're game.

This collection of cocktail recipes may not contain rum, but there's no reason why they can't stand side-by-side among the tiki greats. Pour them in a tiki mug, add an outrageously over-the-top garnish and – even better – serve them under the sun on a balmy day, and you'll infuse them with the spirit of tiki.

Whether you prefer other spirits, feel like something different or just want to give rum a rest, give these fun, fruity tipples a spin every now and then.

FROZEN MARGARITA

A stone-cold winner on a sizzling summer's day, sip slowly to avoid brain freeze.

SERVES 1

2 oz (60 ml) tequila
½ oz (15 ml) Cointreau
⅔ oz (20 ml) freshly squeezed lime juice
⅔ oz (20 ml) freshly squeezed lemon juice
½ oz (15 ml) Sugar syrup (page 250)
salt and lime wheel, for garnish

Place the ingredients (except the garnish)
in a high-speed blender with 1 cup ice. Blend at high
speed until smooth.

Pour into a chilled cocktail glass rimmed with salt.

Garnish with a lime wheel.

MARGARITA

Perfect the balance between sweet, salty and sour, and you'll have plenty of friends lining up to savor your masterful margarita mixing skills.

SERVES 1

1½ oz (45 ml) tequila

½ oz (15 ml) Cointreau

1 oz (30 ml) freshly squeezed lime juice

¼ oz (7.5 ml) Sugar syrup (page 250)

salt and lime wedge, for garnish

Combine the ingredients (except the garnish) in a cocktail shaker filled with ice. Shake.

Strain into a chilled cocktail glass rimmed with salt.

Garnish with a lime wedge.

EL BURRO MARGARITA

This cocktail's chili and tequila combo can feel just like a kick from a donkey. Proceed with caution.

SERVES 1

2¾ oz (½ cup) chopped pineapple
3 sprigs cilantro (coriander)
1½ oz (45 ml) tequila
½ oz (15 ml) Cointreau
1 oz (30 ml) freshly squeezed lime juice
½ oz (15 ml) Sugar syrup (page 250)
2 dashes hot sauce
salt, lime wedge and chili powder, for garnish

Muddle the pineapple and cilantro in a cocktail shaker. Add the remaining ingredients (except the garnish) and fill the shaker with ice. Shake vigorously.

Strain into a chilled cocktail glass rimmed with salt.

Garnish with a lime wedge and a sprinkle of chili powder.

PASSIONFRUIT MARGARITA

*After your guests have recovered
from the visual spectacle of the flaming
passionfruit garnish, they'll be bowled
over by the zesty, sweet flavor of
this speciality margarita.*

SERVES 1

1½ oz (45 ml) tequila
½ oz (15 ml) Cointreau
pulp from 1 passionfruit (reserve ½ shell)
1 oz (30 ml) freshly squeezed lime juice
½ oz (15 ml) Passionfruit syrup (page 256)
½ oz (15 ml) green chartreuse

Combine the tequila, Cointreau, passionfruit pulp,
lime juice and passionfruit syrup in a cocktail
shaker filled with ice. Shake.

Strain into an old fashioned glass filled with ice.

Place the reserved passionfruit shell on top of the
drink, pour in the chartreuse and carefully ignite.

WOODPECKER

*Brazil's favorite spirit
may form the base of this
flighty refreshment, but it's Italian
Galliano that elevates this cocktail
to the next level.*

SERVES 1

**2 oz (60 ml) cachaça
2½ oz (75 ml) freshly squeezed orange juice
½ oz (15 ml) freshly squeezed lime juice
⅓ oz (10 ml) Sugar syrup (page 250)
½ oz (15 ml) Galliano
orange wheel and lime wedge,
for garnish**

Combine the cachaça, fruit juices and sugar syrup in a cocktail shaker filled with ice. Shake.

Strain into an old fashioned glass filled with crushed ice. Float the Galliano on top by pouring it over the back of a spoon.

Garnish with an orange wheel and a lime wedge.

SATURN

*A cocktail so good its creator
took home the 1967 International Bartender's
Association World Championship; this somewhat
simple gin tipple is out-of-this-world good.*

SERVES 1

1½ oz (45 ml) gin
½ oz (15 ml) freshly squeezed lemon juice
⅙ oz (5 ml) Passionfruit syrup (page 256)
⅙ oz (5 ml) Orgeat syrup (page 252)
⅙ oz (5 ml) Velvet falernum (page 257)
mint sprig and lemon wheel, for garnish

Place the ingredients (except the garnish) in
a high-speed blender with 1 cup ice. Blend at
high speed for 5 seconds.

Pour into a highball glass and garnish with mint
and a lemon wheel.

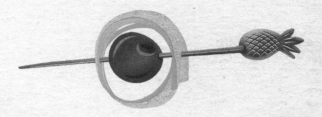

PINEAPPLE NEGRONI

*The Italian icon gets the tiki treatment.
Sophisticated sippers will appreciate this
bittersweet beauty.*

SERVES 1

1 oz (30 ml) pineapple rum
1 oz (30 ml) Campari
1 oz (30 ml) sweet vermouth
pineapple wedge, for garnish

Combine the ingredients (except the garnish) in
an old fashioned glass filled with ice. Stir.

Garnish with a pineapple wedge.

LAKA'S NECTAR

A homage to the Hawaiian goddess of Hula, drink a few of these and you'll be dancing in no time.

SERVES 1

1½ oz (45 ml) silver mezcal
½ oz (15 ml) white rum
½ oz (15 ml) agave nectar
2 oz (60 ml) ginger beer
hibiscus flower, for garnish

Combine the mezcal, rum and agave nectar in a cocktail shaker filled with ice. Shake.

Strain into a highball glass filled with ice. Top with ginger beer and garnish with a hibiscus flower.

GONE NATIVE

Pimm's, gin, apple, lemon and guava is a combination you may not have thought of before, but you'll be glad someone else has, once you try this one.

SERVES 1

1½ oz (45 ml) gin
½ oz (15 ml) Pimm's No. 1
1 oz (30 ml) guava juice
½ oz (15 ml) freshly squeezed lemon juice
1 oz (30 ml) cloudy apple juice
mint sprig and guava slices, for garnish

Combine the ingredients (except the garnish) in a cocktail shaker filled with ice. Shake.

Strain into a highball glass filled with ice and garnish with mint and guava slices.

HO'OPONO POTION

Your reward for learning to pronounce this cocktail name is a bittersweet thirst-quencher. The inclusion of muddled cucumber really amps up the refreshment factor.

SERVES 1

4 slices cucumber, plus extra for garnish
1½ oz (45 ml) silver tequila
½ oz (15 ml) Aperol
1 oz (30 ml) freshly squeezed lime juice
⅔ oz (20 ml) Sugar syrup (page 250)

Muddle the cucumber slices (except the garnish) in a cocktail shaker. Add the other ingredients and fill the shaker with ice. Shake vigorously.

Strain into an old fashioned glass and add a large ice cube.

Garnish with a cucumber slice.

TROTSKY

Ever drunk an alcoholic drink out of a dainty teacup? Featuring chilled Caravan tea spiked with Russian vodka, this cocktail will certainly spice up your next afternoon tea.

SERVES 1

2 oz (60 ml) Russian vodka
⅔ oz (20 ml) freshly squeezed lemon juice
⅔ oz (20 ml) Honey syrup (page 253)
4 oz (120 ml) Russian Caravan tea, chilled
lemon slices, for garnish

Combine the ingredients (except the garnish) in a teapot filled with ice and stir.

Serve in tea cups with a wedge of lemon.

AGENT ORANGE

A cocktail named after a dangerous herbicide famously used in warfare is every bit as serious as you'd expect. This one is strictly for seasoned drinkers who can handle their booze.

SERVES 1

½ oz (15 ml) tequila
½ oz (15 ml) vodka
½ oz (15 ml) dark rum
½ oz (15 ml) white rum
½ oz (15 ml) orange curaçao
2 oz (60 ml) freshly squeezed orange juice
⅓ oz (10 ml) green chartreuse

Combine the ingredients (except the chartreuse) in a cocktail shaker filled with ice. Shake.

Strain into a highball glass filled with ice.

Float the chartreuse on top by pouring it over the back of a spoon and carefully igniting it.

MEXICAN HEADHUNTER

Honey, ginger, sage and tequila may seem like a curious combination, but one sip will set your head straight.

SERVES 1

3 sage leaves
1 oz (30 ml) reposado tequila
1 oz (30 ml) añejo tequila
⅙ oz (5 ml) ginger liqueur
⅔ oz (20 ml) freshly squeezed lemon juice
½ oz (15 ml) Sugar syrup (page 250)
½ oz (15 ml) Honey syrup (page 253)
2 dashes Orange bitters (page 258)
mint and pineapple wedge, for garnish

Lightly muddle the sage leaves in a cocktail shaker. Add the remaining ingredients (except the garnish) and fill the shaker with ice. Shake vigorously.

Pour the contents of the shaker into a highball glass. Garnish with mint and a pineapple wedge.

HONI HONI

*This Trader Vic's classic
means "to kiss" in Hawaiian.
Drink one and you'll be
puckering up for more.*

SERVES 1

2 oz (60 ml) bourbon

½ oz (15 ml) orange curaçao

1 oz (30 ml) freshly squeezed lime juice

½ oz (15 ml) Orgeat syrup (page 252)

maraschino cherry and pineapple wedge,
for garnish

Combine the ingredients (except the garnish) in
a cocktail shaker filled with ice. Shake.

Strain into an old fashioned glass filled with crushed
ice. Garnish with a maraschino cherry and a
pineapple wedge.

SUFFERING BASTARD

Proving that necessity really is the mother of invention, this historic drink was first made in Cairo during World War Two. Liquor was hard to come by, so gin borrowed from the postal exchange, brandy from Cyprus and bitters from a local chemist had to do.

SERVES 1

1 oz (30 ml) brandy or cognac
1 oz (30 ml) gin
½ oz (15 ml) ginger liqueur
½ oz (15 ml) freshly squeezed lime juice
2 oz (60 ml) ginger beer
3 dashes Orange bitters (page 258)
lime wedge, for garnish

Combine the liquor and lime juice in a cocktail shaker filled with ice. Shake.

Strain into a highball glass filled with crushed ice and top with ginger beer.

Add the bitters and garnish with a lime wedge.

CHI CHI

This Piña Colada-adjacent blended
cocktail tastes like paradise –
namely, pineapple, coconut,
sugar and vodka.

SERVES 1

2 oz (60 ml) vodka
3½ oz (100 ml) pineapple juice, fresh
if possible
⅔ oz (20 ml) coconut cream
½ oz (15 ml) Sugar syrup (page 250)
½ oz (15 ml) Orgeat syrup (page 252)
pineapple wedge and cocktail umbrella,
for garnish

Place the ingredients (except the garnish)
in a high-speed blender with 1½ cups crushed
ice. Blend until smooth.

Pour into a poco grande glass and
garnish with a pineapple wedge
and cocktail umbrella.

SINGAPORE SLING

Created by Ngiam Tong Boon sometime around 1915, this iconic cocktail is synonymous with Singapore's Raffles Hotel. More than a century later, tourists still flock to the hotel bar to order it.

SERVES 1

1 oz (30 ml) gin
1 oz (30 ml) cherry brandy
1 oz (30 ml) orange curaçao
1 oz (30 ml) freshly squeezed lime juice
2 oz (60 ml) soda water
2 dashes Orange bitters (page 258)
maraschino cherry, for garnish

Pour the gin, cherry brandy, curaçao and lime juice into a highball glass filled with ice cubes. Top with the soda.

Add the bitters and garnish with a maraschino cherry.

BOOZY
BORA BORA

Dreaming of an overwater bungalow stay? Bring Bora Bora to your abode by mixing this delicious gin cocktail as a consolation prize.

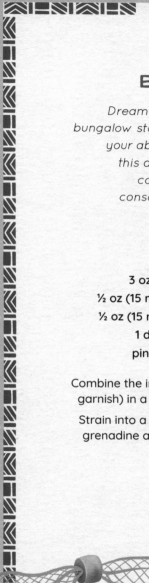

SERVES 1

1½ oz (45 ml) gin
3 oz (90 ml) cloudy apple juice
½ oz (15 ml) Passionfruit syrup (page 256)
½ oz (15 ml) freshly squeezed lemon juice
1 dash Grenadine (page 251)
pineapple wedge, for garnish

Combine the ingredients (except the grenadine and garnish) in a cocktail shaker filled with ice. Shake.

Strain into a highball glass filled with ice. Add the grenadine and garnish with a pineapple wedge.

CAIPIRINHA

It only takes a few ingredients to whip up Brazil's national cocktail, which is fortuitous because one Caipirinha is never enough.

SERVES 1

1 lime, cut into 12 pieces
1 tablespoon soft brown sugar
2 oz (60 ml) cachaça
lime wheel, for garnish

Muddle the lime and sugar in a cocktail shaker. Add the cachaça and fill the shaker with ice. Shake vigorously.

Pour the contents of the shaker into an old fashioned glass and garnish with a lime wheel.

ILLUSION SHAKER

This green machine had a moment in nightclubs in the 90s. Add some authenticity to your next 90s-themed party by serving a few of these bad boys.

SERVES 1

1 oz (30 ml) melon liqueur

1½ oz (45 ml) vodka

½ oz (15 ml) coconut rum

½ oz (15 ml) Cointreau or triple sec

1½ oz (45 ml) pineapple juice, fresh if possible

Combine the ingredients in a cocktail shaker filled with ice. Shake.

MINT JULEP

Low on ingredients? Bourbon and mint are all you need to make this refreshing cocktail associated with the Kentucky Derby.

SERVES 1

4 mint leaves
½ oz (15 ml) mint syrup
2 oz (60 ml) bourbon
mint sprigs, for garnish

Muddle the mint leaves in a metal cup. Add the syrup and bourbon and stir to combine.

Fill the cup with crushed ice and garnish with fresh mint.

COSMOPOLITAN

*This pretty, pink cocktail rode
a wave of popularity in the early 2000s
thanks to its association with Sex and the City.
Just like New York City's residents, the
Cosmo has real staying power.*

SERVES 1

1 oz (30 ml) vodka
1 oz (30 ml) Cointreau or triple sec
1 oz (30 ml) cranberry juice
½ oz (15 ml) freshly squeezed lime juice
lemon, lime or orange twist, for garnish

Combine the ingredients (except the garnish)
in a cocktail shaker filled with ice. Shake.

Strain into a chilled cocktail glass and
garnish with a twist.

SEX ON THE BEACH

Awkward to order, easy to drink.

SERVES 1

1½ oz (45 ml) vodka
½ oz (15 ml) peach schnapps
2 oz (60 ml) cranberry juice
2 oz (60 ml) freshly squeezed orange juice
cocktail umbrella, for garnish

Combine the ingredients in a cocktail shaker
filled with ice. Shake.

Strain into a highball glass filled with ice. Garnish
with a cocktail umbrella.

BLUE LAGOON

*Recreate the 70s vibe in your
own living room with this long, tall drink
of turquoise. Break out the fondue set,
play some Steely Dan and you've
got yourself a party.*

SERVES 1

2 oz (60 ml) vodka
½ oz (15 ml) blue curaçao
3½ oz (100 ml) lemonade
maraschino cherry, for garnish

Combine the vodka and curaçao in a highball glass
filled with ice. Top with with lemonade.

Garnish with a maraschino cherry.

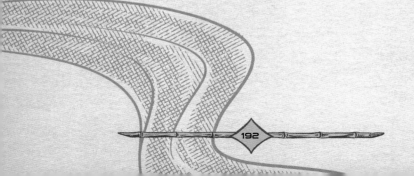

WHISKEY SOUR

Getting the balance right is paramount when mixing this classy tipple. Experiment with a variety of whiskey brands and this one will taste different every time. It's pretty much a cocktail that keeps giving.

SERVES 1

2 oz (60 ml) whiskey
1⅓ oz (40 ml) freshly squeezed lemon juice
⅔ oz (20 ml) Sugar syrup (page 250)
1 egg white
maraschino cherry, for garnish

Combine the ingredients (except the garnish) in a cocktail shaker filled with ice and shake vigorously.

Strain into an old fashioned glass filled with ice. Garnish with a maraschino cherry.

AMARETTO SOUR

A riff on the whiskey sour, this classic cocktail has a slight nutty taste thanks to the addition of the Italian liqueur, amaretto. Stick with the European theme by garnishing with a maraschino cherry. Salut!

SERVES 1

2 oz (60 ml) amaretto
1⅓ oz (40 ml) freshly squeezed lemon juice
⅔ oz (20 ml) Orgeat syrup (page 252)
1 egg white
maraschino cherry, for garnish

Combine the ingredients (except the garnish) in a cocktail shaker filled with ice and shake vigorously.

Strain into an old fashioned glass filled with ice.

Garnish with a maraschino cherry.

SALTY SEA DOG

In the cocktail world, looks can be deceiving. This drink may look a little "sugar and spice and all things nice," but a salted rim gives this blush-pink cocktail a savory edge.

SERVES 1

1 oz (30 ml) tequila

½ oz (15 ml) Campari

2 oz (60 ml) freshly squeezed pink grapefruit juice

salt, pink grapefruit slice and cocktail umbrella, for garnish

Combine the ingredients (except the garnish) in an old fashioned glass rimmed with salt and filled with ice.

Garnish with a pink grapefruit slice and a cocktail umbrella.

PIMM'S CUP

A cocktail that's been sold at the Wimbledon tennis tournament since the 1970s, this classy tipple favored by the Brits is fruity enough to be given the tiki treatment.

SERVES 1

1 oz (30 ml) gin
1½ oz (45 ml) Pimm's No. 1
slices of cucumber, apple, orange, lemon, lime
6 mint leaves
3 oz (90 ml) ginger ale

Combine the ingredients in a highball glass filled with ice and stir.

PINK LADY

*This Prohibition-era creation is
a gin-forward cocktail perfect for people
who gravitate toward more
crowd-pleasing tipples.*

SERVES 1

2 oz (60 ml) gin
½ oz (15 ml) Cointreau or triple sec
1 oz (30 ml) freshly squeezed lemon juice
¼ oz (7.5 ml) Grenadine (page 251)
lemon twist, for garnish

Combine the ingredients (except the garnish) in
a cocktail shaker filled with ice. Shake.

Strain into a chilled cocktail glass. Garnish with
a lemon twist.

PEACH AND GINGER COBBLER

Can't decide if you want dessert or a drink? Why not have both?

SERVES 1

2 oz (60 ml) rye whiskey

⅓ oz (10 ml) ginger liqueur

2 oz (60 ml) peach nectar

½ oz (15 ml) Orgeat syrup (page 252)

1 dash Orange bitters (page 258)

4 fresh mint leaves, chopped

½ oz (15 ml) freshly squeezed lemon juice

½ peach, stone removed

⅙ oz (5 ml) soft brown sugar

⅓ oz (10 ml) 151 proof rum

Combine the whiskey, ginger liqueur, peach nectar, orgeat syrup, bitters, mint and lemon juice in a cocktail shaker filled with ice. Shake.

Strain into a large old fashioned glass filled with ice.

Place the peach in the top of the drink, cut side up. Fill the cavity with the sugar and rum and carefully ignite.

SHIRLEY TEMPLE, ALL GROWN UP

A boozy version of the famous mocktail named for the original child movie star, you'll be sailing on the Good Ship Lollipop after downing a few of these.

SERVES 1

2 oz (60 ml) vodka
½ oz (15 ml) freshly squeezed lime juice
3 oz (90 ml) ginger beer
½ oz (15 ml) Grenadine (page 251)
1 tablespoon passionfruit pulp
orange wheel, for garnish

Pour the vodka and lime juice into a highball glass filled with ice and top with the ginger beer. Stir.

Slowly add the grenadine, pouring against the inside of the glass so that it sinks to the bottom. Spoon the passionfruit pulp on top and garnish with an orange wheel.

LA BAMBA

*Featuring coconut, cherry
and cream, this is the gourmet candy
bar of the cocktail world.*

SERVES 1

1½ oz (45 ml) cachaça
1 oz (30 ml) coconut rum
½ oz (15 ml) maraschino cherry liqueur
½ oz (15 ml) maraschino cherry juice
1½ oz (45 ml) cream
maraschino cherry, for garnish

Combine the ingredients (except the garnish)
in a cocktail shaker filled with ice. Shake.

Strain into a chilled cocktail glass and garnish
with a maraschino cherry.

PINE-LIME SPLICE

*Coconut rum, melon liqueur
and pineapple juice combine to
create this refreshing, green and gold
pick-me-up. Add a beach sunset and a
slight breeze and you've got yourself
the ultimate summer set-up.*

SERVES 1

1 oz (30 ml) vodka
1 oz (30 ml) coconut rum
1 oz (30 ml) melon liqueur
3 oz (90 ml) pineapple juice, fresh if possible
1 oz (30 ml) cream
pineapple wedge and pineapple leaves,
for garnish

Combine the vodka, rum and liqueur in a poco grande
glass filled with ice. Top with pineapple juice, ensuring
that there's some room left at the top.

Float the cream on top by pouring it over the back
of a spoon.

Garnish with a pineapple wedge and pineapple leaves.

PISCO
IN THE SNOW

*Take a trip to South America
without getting on a plane by mixing
up this tart, tangy burst of
sunshine in a glass.*

SERVES 1

1 oz (30 ml) white rum
½ oz (15 ml) freshly squeezed lemon juice
⅔ oz (20 ml) Passionfruit syrup (page 256)
1 oz (30 ml) pisco brandy
lemon twist, for garnish

Combine the rum, lemon juice and passionfruit
syrup in a cocktail shaker filled with ice. Shake.

Strain into an old fashioned glass and fill
with crushed ice.

Pour pisco brandy into the center of the ice
and garnish with a lemon twist.

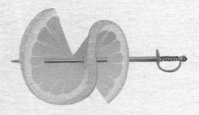

CACTUS COLADA

*Celebrate Cinco de Mayo
with this tequila-spiked version of
the Piña Colada. Add some tamales
and you're onto a winner.*

SERVES 1

2 oz (60 ml) tequila
½ oz (15 ml) coconut rum
⅓ oz (10 ml) Orgeat syrup (page 252)
1 oz (30 ml) pineapple juice, fresh if possible
1 oz (30 ml) freshly squeezed orange juice
⅓ oz (10 ml) Grenadine (page 251)
⅔ oz (20 ml) coconut cream
opened coconut, for serving (optional)

Place the ingredients in a high-speed blender filled
with ice. Blend at high speed until smooth.

Pour into a coconut (or a large cocktail glass)
and top with crushed ice.

TEQUILA SUNRISE

*A 1970s cocktail classic favored
by Rolling Stones frontman Mick Jagger.
If it's good enough for rock royalty...*

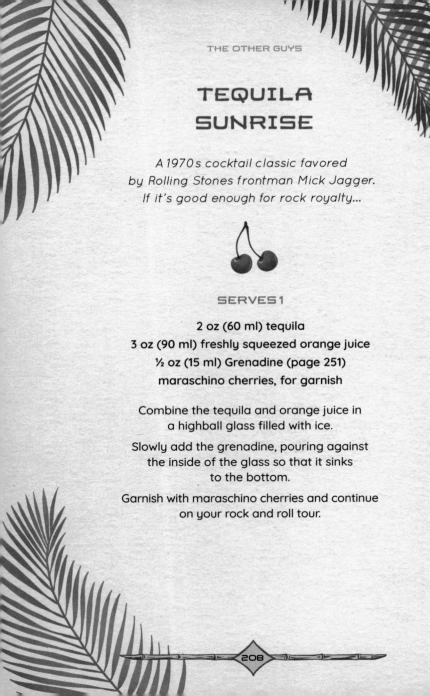

SERVES 1

2 oz (60 ml) tequila
3 oz (90 ml) freshly squeezed orange juice
½ oz (15 ml) Grenadine (page 251)
maraschino cherries, for garnish

Combine the tequila and orange juice in
a highball glass filled with ice.

Slowly add the grenadine, pouring against
the inside of the glass so that it sinks
to the bottom.

Garnish with maraschino cherries and continue
on your rock and roll tour.

CARIBBEAN SUNRISE

The Tequila Sunrise's cousin from the Caribbean moves this cocktail closer to its tiki origins.

SERVES 1

2 oz (60 ml) Caribbean rum

3 oz (90 ml) freshly squeezed orange juice

½ oz (15 ml) Grenadine (page 251)

pineapple wedge, for garnish

Combine the rum and orange juice in a highball glass filled with ice.

Slowly add the grenadine, pouring against the inside of the glass so that it sinks to the bottom.

Garnish with a pineapple wedge.

RASPBERRY GIN RICKEY

The best chefs make the most of seasonal ingredients, as do bartenders. Celebrate berry season by mixing up this effervescent gin treat that champions the season's best.

SERVES 4

13 oz (3 cups) fresh raspberries,
plus extra for garnish
4 oz (½ cup) sugar
4 oz (120 ml) freshly squeezed lime juice
8 oz (240 ml) gin
soda water, for topping
lime wedges, for garnish

Place the raspberries, sugar and lime juice in a small jug and muddle gently. Add the gin and leave to steep at room temperature for 2–3 hours, stirring occasionally.

When ready to serve, pour into old fashioned glasses filled with ice and top with soda.

Garnish with fresh raspberries and lime wedges.

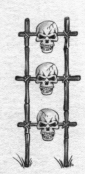

BITTER AND TWISTED

*With a slightly bitter tang
and a twisty garnish,
this blood orange-
heavy cocktail lives
up to its name.*

SERVES 1

1 oz (30 ml) gin
1 oz (30 ml) Campari
1 oz (30 ml) red vermouth
2 oz (60 ml) freshly squeezed blood orange juice
blood orange twist, for garnish

Combine the ingredients (except the garnish) in
an old fashioned glass filled with ice.

Garnish with a blood orange twist.

THE
BEE KEEPER

Apart from soothing a sore throat, this tasty honey-lemon number spiked with cognac and orange curaçao will give you a slight buzz. But what else would you expect from a cocktail with a name like The Bee Keeper?

SERVES 1

1½ oz (45 ml) cognac
1 oz (30 ml) orange curaçao
1 oz (30 ml) freshly squeezed lemon juice
½ oz (15 ml) Honey syrup (page 253)
lemon wheel, for garnish

Combine the ingredients (except the garnish) in a cocktail shaker filled with ice. Shake.

Strain into a chilled cocktail glass and garnish with a lemon wheel.

BLOODY GOOD BLOODY MARY

The breakfast of champions known for taking the edge off a night of heavy drinking, this savory brunch favorite is both a meal and a hangover cure in one.

SERVES 1

1½ oz (45 ml) vodka
⅓ oz (10 ml) dry sherry
⅓ oz (10 ml) rich red wine
⅚ oz (25 ml) freshly squeezed lemon juice
few generous dashes hot sauce
pinch of celery salt
freshly ground black pepper
3 oz (90 ml) good-quality tomato juice
pickled chili, dill pickle, barbecued shrimp (prawn) and celery stalk, for garnish

Combine the vodka, sherry, wine, lemon juice, hot sauce, celery salt and pepper in a large glass. Stir. Fill with ice and top with the tomato juice.

Check the flavor and adjust to taste.

Thread a chili, dill pickle and shrimp onto a long skewer and place into the drink along with a celery stalk.

TIGER LILLET

If you've never heard of Lillet, you're missing out. Get acquainted with this French wine-based apertif by whipping up this four-ingredient, aromatic cocktail that's the perfect tipple to kick off a sophisticated cocktail party or dinner.

SERVES 1

2 oz (60 ml) Lillet Blanc

1 oz (30 ml) Campari

1 oz (30 ml) freshly squeezed pink grapefruit juice

blood orange twist, for garnish

Combine the ingredients (except the garnish) in an old fashioned glass filled with ice.

Garnish with a blood orange twist.

MINT
SPRIG

*A sunny afternoon garden party is
made all the better with this fresh, light cocktail
packed with the green goodness of cucumber and
mint. Extra points if you pick the mint
from your own backyard.*

SERVES 1

2 oz (60 ml) cucumber gin
1 oz (30 ml) freshly squeezed lime juice
⅔ oz (20 ml) Grenadine (page 251)
½ oz (15 ml) Sugar syrup (page 250)
3 oz (90 ml) soda water
mint sprig and cucumber ribbon, for garnish

Combine the ingredients (except the garnish) in a highball
glass filled with crushed ice and stir to combine.

Garnish with mint and a cucumber ribbon.

MONKEY WRENCH

*Add a Monkey Wrench
to your cocktail toolbox (next to the
Screwdriver, of course) and you'll
always have a barrel of fun.*

SERVES 1

1 oz (30 ml) vodka
½ oz (15 ml) coconut rum
2 oz (60 ml) pineapple juice, fresh if possible
2 oz (60 ml) freshly squeezed orange juice
orange wheel and plastic monkey, for garnish

Combine the ingredients (except the garnish) in
a cocktail shaker filled with ice. Shake.

Strain into a highball glass filled with ice.

Garnish with an orange wheel and one of those
little plastic monkeys they used to put on
drinks in the 1980s.

GINGER MEGGS

Named after an Australian comic strip character (think Dennis the Menace, but with red hair), this vodka cocktail featuring ginger, lemon, pineapple and cinnamon, is a little sweet, a little spicy and whole lot of fun.

SERVES 1

1½ oz (45 ml) vodka
½ oz (15 ml) ginger liqueur
1 oz (30 ml) freshly squeezed lemon juice
1 oz (30 ml) pineapple juice, fresh if possible
½ oz (15 ml) Cinnamon syrup (page 255)
pineapple wedge and star anise, for garnish

Combine the ingredients (except the garnish) in a cocktail shaker filled with ice. Shake.

Strain into a highball glass filled with crushed ice. Garnish with a pineapple wedge and star anise.

SMOKE STACK

Each sip of this cocktail will reveal a different flavor as you make your way toward the bottom of the tall glass. Wait for that hint of smoky single malt to hit.

SERVES 1

1 oz (30 ml) Irish whiskey

½ oz (15 ml) ginger liqueur

1 oz (30 ml) freshly squeezed lemon juice

⅔ oz (20 ml) Sugar syrup (page 250)

⅔ oz (20 ml) Honey syrup (page 253)

2 oz (60 ml) soda water

½ oz (15 ml) smoky single malt whisky

Place the Irish whiskey, liqueur, lemon juice and syrups in a high-speed blender with 1 cup crushed ice. Blend at high speed for 5 seconds.

Pour into a highball glass and top with crushed ice and soda.

Float the single malt on top by pouring it over the back of a spoon.

FRUIT TINGLE

Forget the old adage to never drink anything blue and take this sapphire spectacle for a spin if you're in need of a fizzy, sweet sidekick.

SERVES 1

1½ oz (45 ml) vodka
½ oz (15 ml) blue curaçao
3½ oz (100 ml) lemonade
½ oz (15 ml) Grenadine (page 251)
fresh cherries, for garnish

Pour the vodka and blue curaçao into a hurricane glass filled with ice and top with the lemonade. Stir.

Slowly add the grenadine, pouring against the inside of the glass so that it sinks to the bottom.

Garnish with cherries.

FROZEN BIKINI

*What happens when you spike
a Bellini and blend it with ice?
You get this summery take
on an Italian icon.*

SERVES 1

1 oz (30 ml) vodka
½ oz (15 ml) peach schnapps
1 oz (30 ml) peach nectar
3 oz (90 ml) sparkling white wine, chilled
strawberry, for garnish

Place the vodka, schnapps and nectar
in a high-speed blender with 1 cup ice and blend
at high speed until smooth.

Pour into a chilled champagne flute and top
with sparkling wine.

Garnish with a strawberry.

HONOLULU

*Just like Hawaii's capital,
this gin cocktail has a way of
helping people relax.*

SERVES 1

2 oz (60 ml) gin
½ oz (15 ml) pineapple juice, fresh if possible
⅓ oz (10 ml) freshly squeezed lemon juice
2 dashes Orange bitters (page 258)
sugar and lemon wheel, for garnish

Combine the ingredients (except the garnish) in a cocktail shaker filled with ice. Shake.

Strain into a chilled cocktail glass rimmed with sugar. Garnish with a lemon wheel.

PUNCH BOWLS

From a dramatic flaming volcano to a fizzy, fruity mix served in a dainty vintage crystal bowl, nothing brings people together like a punch bowl. Whether it's a games night, frat party, backyard wedding or fancy dinner with friends, punch makes every event better.

These recipes can be made for four or forty people, depending on how many friends you have (or want to have) around you. The best part is that almost anything can be used as a punch bowl. You could go all-out and invest in an ornate ceramic tiki bowl, pick up an old-school crystal bowl from a thrift store, or simply use a salad bowl, basin, bath or any vessel that will hold gallons of fruit, juice, ice, alcohol and soda.

There aren't many hard and fast rules with punch, so get creative and produce the perfect punch bowl for your next party.

SCORPION BOWL

This masterpiece created by Donn Beach is a bona fide party starter. For the ultimate authentic experience, gather round and use straws to drink straight from the ceramic bowl. Just make sure the fire is out beforehand, lest you lose an eyebrow!

SERVES 5-10

10 oz (300 ml) dark rum

2 oz (60 ml) brandy or cognac

3 oz (90 ml) Orgeat syrup (page 252)

4 oz (120 ml) freshly squeezed lemon juice

3 oz (90 ml) freshly squeezed orange juice

3 oz (90 ml) pineapple juice, fresh if possible

3 oz (90 ml) guava juice

cinnamon sticks, edible flowers and lime slices, for garnish

squeezed lime half

½ oz (15 ml) 151 proof rum

Place the ingredients (except the garnish, lime half and 151 proof rum) in a high-speed blender with ½ cup crushed ice. Blend until smooth.

Pour into a scorpion bowl or other large punch bowl and add blocks of ice. Garnish with cinnamon sticks, edible flowers and lime slices.

Invert the lime half so that the skin side creates a cup. Place it in the center of the scorpion bowl or float it in the punch. Fill the lime cup with 151 proof rum and carefully ignite.

PLANTER'S PUNCH BOWL

A party-sized version of an old school American cocktail (featured on page 28), you'll need both white and dark rum to pull off this punch bowl.

SERVES 5–10

5 oz (150 ml) dark rum
5 oz (150 ml) white rum
3 oz (90 ml) orange curaçao
6 oz (180 ml) freshly squeezed orange juice
3 oz (90 ml) freshly squeezed lime juice
3 oz (90 ml) Sugar syrup (page 250)
½ oz (15 ml) Allspice dram (page 259)
3 oz (90 ml) Grenadine (page 251)
1 tablespoon Orange bitters (page 258)
pineapple pieces, orange and lime wheels, for garnish

Combine the ingredients (except the garnish) in a large punch bowl with large blocks of ice. Chill for 2–4 hours.

Add more ice and garnish with pineapple pieces and orange and lime wheels.

HURRICANE PUNCH

*Blow your guests away
with this group-size version
of the 1940s New Orleans classic.
Hold onto your hats, there's a
lot of rum in this one!*

SERVES 10

12 oz (350 ml) dark rum

12 oz (350 ml) white rum

10 oz (300 ml) freshly squeezed orange juice

10 oz (300 ml) pineapple juice, fresh if possible

10 oz (300 ml) freshly squeezed lime juice

5 oz (150 ml) passionfruit juice

1 oz (30 ml) Orgeat syrup (page 252)

1 oz (30 ml) Grenadine (page 251)

orange wheels and maraschino cherries,
for garnish

Combine the ingredients (except the garnish) in
a large punch bowl with large blocks of ice.
Chill for 2–4 hours.

Add more ice and garnish with orange wheels
and maraschino cherries.

TAHITIAN RUM PUNCH

Dating all the way back to 1934, this Donn Beach creation has real staying power. Packed with fruit juices, you'll get a good dose of vitamin C with every sip.

SERVES 10-20

1 lb (450 g) soft brown sugar
32 oz (4 cups) white rum
24 oz (3 cups) dark rum
1 bottle dry white or sparkling wine
32 oz (4 cups) freshly squeezed orange juice
32 oz (4 cups) freshly squeezed grapefruit juice
32 oz (4 cups) pineapple juice, fresh if possible
16 oz (2 cups) freshly squeezed lime juice
2 oz (60 ml) Vanilla syrup (page 254)
3 bananas, 6 oranges and 3 grapefruit, cut into slices
1 pineapple, cored and cut into chunks
pineapple leaves, star fruit slices and maraschino cherries, for garnish

Combine the sugar with 8 oz (1 cup) water in a large saucepan over medium-high heat, stirring until the sugar is dissolved. Set aside to cool.

In a very large punch bowl, combine the brown sugar syrup with the rest of the ingredients (except the garnish) and large blocks of ice. Allow to chill overnight.

Garnish with pineapple leaves, star fruit and maraschino cherries.

VOODOO JUICE

What happens when you combine five different types of rum with three different kinds of fruit juice? You get this powerful punch guaranteed to get the party started.

SERVES 20-30

24 oz (3 cups) coconut rum

24 oz (3 cups) banana rum

24 oz (3 cups) pineapple rum

24 oz (3 cups) orange rum

24 oz (3 cups) spiced rum

64 oz (8 cups) cranberry juice

64 oz (8 cups) freshly squeezed orange juice

64 oz (8 cups) pineapple juice, fresh if possible

pineapple pieces and orange, banana, lemon and lime slices, for garnish

Combine the ingredients (except the garnish) in a very large punch bowl along with large blocks of ice.

Allow to chill overnight. Garnish with the pineapple pieces and fruit slices.

TONGA PUNCH

A pretty punch garnished with edible flowers, this lighter-style punch will infuse your next gathering with a touch of floral elegance.

SERVES 15-20

32 oz (4 cups) white rum
10 oz (300 ml) orange curaçao
32 oz (4 cups) freshly squeezed orange juice
16 oz (2 cups) freshly squeezed lemon juice
5 oz (150 ml) freshly squeezed lime juice
3½ oz (105 ml) Grenadine (page 251)
edible flowers, for garnish

Combine the ingredients (except the garnish) in a large punch bowl with large blocks of ice. Chill for 2–4 hours.

Add more ice and garnish with edible flowers.

EUREKA PUNCH

A punch and pyrotechnic display in one, light a match and set this baby alight to add some visual drama to your next get together.

SERVES 30-40

48 oz (6 cups) aged rum
20 oz (600 ml) yellow chartreuse
32 oz (4 cups) Honey syrup (page 253)
48 oz (6 cups) freshly squeezed lemon juice
1 oz (30 ml) Orange bitters (page 258)
80 oz (10 cups) ginger ale
mint sprigs, lemon wheels and edible flowers, for garnish

In a large container, combine the rum, chartreuse, honey syrup, lemon juice and bitters with large blocks of ice and 8 oz (1 cup) iced water. Chill for at least 2 hours.

Serve in several punch bowls, or one enormous vessel. Top with ginger ale, ice and garnish with mint, lemon wheels and edible flowers.

This drink can be set on fire due to the large quantity of yellow chartreuse. If you wish to do so, first ensure your punch is in a heat proof vessel. Light a match then, using a long-handled metal spoon, pick up a spoonful of the punch. Bring the spoon to the match to light, then carefully bring the lit spoon to the punch bowl. Make sure you're standing back when it ignites, and use a large saucepan lid or a frying pan to extinguish the flame.

FISH HOUSE PUNCH

The first known record of this punch can be tracked back to 1744, in a Philadelphia fishing club known as The Fish House. There are two different varieties of tea and a whole cup of sugar in this one, but as the oldest recipe in the book, people did things different back then.

SERVES 10-20

peeled rind of 4 lemons
8 oz (1 cup) sugar
16 oz (2 cups) warm English Breakfast tea
16 oz (2 cups) warm Earl Grey tea
8 oz (1 cup) freshly squeezed lemon juice
32 oz (4 cups) dark rum
16 oz (2 cups) brandy or cognac
4 oz (120 ml) peach brandy
lemon wheels and freshly grated nutmeg, for garnish

In a large punch bowl, rub the lemon rind and sugar together to release the oils from the rind.
Allow to infuse for 1 hour.

Pour the teas into the bowl and stir until the sugar is dissolved. Add the lemon juice and liquor, and stir to combine.

Add a very large block of ice, then continue to add smaller blocks of ice to achieve the desired dilution.

Garnish with lemon wheels and nutmeg.

KOOKOO CACHAÇA

You don't always need to add a bunch of different alcohol varieties to be onto something good. Sometimes, one spirit is enough and when it comes to punch, you can't go wrong with cachaça.

SERVES 6

32 oz (4 cups) cachaça

16 oz (2 cups) pineapple vodka

16 oz (2 cups) freshly squeezed lemon juice

16 oz (2 cups) Grenadine (page 251)

32 oz (4 cups) soda water

pineapple pieces and lemon wheels, for garnish

Combine the ingredients (except the soda water and garnish) in a large punch bowl with large blocks of ice. Chill for 2–4 hours.

When ready to serve, add more ice and top with soda. Garnish with pineapple pieces and lemon wheels.

WATERMELON MARGARITA

A cool centerpiece for your next summer cookout, this simple punch served in a watermelon proves that it only takes a few ingredients to make a big impact.

SERVES 6-12

1 whole chilled watermelon
24 oz (3 cups) tequila
3 oz (90 ml) freshly squeezed lemon juice
3 oz (90 ml) Sugar syrup (page 250)
grapes, watermelon cubes and cocktail umbrella,
for garnish

Cut a hole in the watermelon big enough to fit in a stick blender. Reserve some pieces for garnish, then puree the flesh inside the watermelon to a juice.

Remove 32 oz (4 cups) watermelon juice and set aside.

Add the tequila, lemon juice and sugar syrup. Stir to combine and top up with watermelon juice as required.

Chill until ready to serve. Garnish with grapes, watermelon cubes and a cocktail umbrella.

THE
SEAWARD

*If coconut and pineapple are
a match made in heaven, then
prepare to reach nirvana with
this moreish, tropical punch.*

SERVES 6-12

32 oz (4 cups) spiced rum
16 oz (2 cups) Grand Marnier
16 oz (2 cups) coconut rum
64 oz (8 cups) pineapple juice, fresh if possible
16 oz (2 cups) freshly squeezed orange juice
16 oz (2 cups) coconut cream
pineapple wedge and shaved coconut,
for garnish

Combine the liquor and juices in a large punch bowl with
large blocks of ice. Chill for 2–4 hours.

When ready to serve, add more ice and top with
coconut cream. Stir to combine.

Garnish with a pineapple wedge and
shaved coconut.

FUN IN
THE SHRUBBS

Want to make a punch that will keep your guests guessing? The secret ingredient in this one is aromatic Creole Shrubb rum from Martinque, which is a bit like liquid gold.

SERVES 6–12

32 oz (4 cups) dark rum

16 oz (2 cups) Creole Shrubb rum

16 oz (2 cups) freshly squeezed lime juice

4 dashes angostura bitters

4 dashes Orange bitters (page 258)

10 oz (300 ml) Sugar syrup (page 250)

lime and orange wheels, for garnish

Combine the ingredients (except the garnish) in a large punch bowl with large blocks of ice. Chill for 2–4 hours.

When ready to serve, add more ice and garnish with lime and orange wheels.

COOK ISLAND CUCKOLD

A fun, fruity, fizzy treat that doesn't overwhelm the palate like some of the boozier punches, this effervescent creation is real crowd pleaser.

SERVES 10-15

32 oz (4 cups) vodka
64 oz (8 cups) pineapple juice, fresh if possible
8 oz (1 cup) cranberry juice
1 bottle sparkling wine, chilled
pineapple pieces, strawberry halves and
lemon wheels, for garnish

Combine the vodka and fruit juices in a large punch bowl with large blocks of ice. Chill for 2–4 hours.

When ready to serve, top with the sparkling wine and more ice.

Garnish with the pineapple pieces, strawberries and lemon wheels.

PASSION PUNCH

The rare inclusion of dry cider makes this recipe a bit of an oddity. If you're passionate about apple cider, this punch delivers.

SERVES 10

32 oz (4 cups) lemon vodka
16 oz (2 cups) guava juice
24 oz (3 cups) cloudy apple juice
8 oz (1 cup) Passionfruit syrup (page 256)
32 oz (4 cups) dry hard cider
pineapple pieces and lime wheels, for garnish.

Combine the vodka, fruit juices and syrup in a large punch bowl with large blocks of ice. Chill for 2–4 hours.

When ready to serve, top with the cider and more ice.

Garnish with pineapple pieces and lime wheels.

PEACH MIMOSA

Every event is made better by a bit of fizz. The ideal punch to serve at a pre-lunch gathering, this punch has boozy bachelorette brunch written all over it.

SERVES 8-10

16 oz (2 cups) peach nectar
8 oz (1 cup) freshly squeezed orange juice
3 oz (90 ml) Grenadine (page 251)
1 bottle sparkling wine

Chill all of your ingredients and champagne flutes completely before starting.

In a small jug, combine the peach nectar, orange juice and grenadine. Stir to combine.

Evenly distribute among chilled champagne flutes and top with sparkling wine.

SYRUPS, BATTERS AND BITTERS

At Don the Beachcomber's, the original tiki bar, they did away with convenience in favor of crafting all their own secret mixes of syrups, batters and bitters. Donn Beach was so protective of his recipes, even the bartenders were kept in the dark as to what was in a lot of the mixers.

Over the years, many bartenders have tried to crack the code of what was in Donn's secret recipes. Yet, decades later the mystery remains for many of them. No one will ever truly know, as Donn died in 1989, taking his knowledge with him.

Sure, there's plenty of mass-produced, pre-made cocktail ingredients you can buy, but learning to make your own syrups, batters and bitters will give your tiki cocktails a winning edge. Not sure how to go about making your own? The basic tiki staples in this chapter are a great place to start perfecting your mixers game.

SUGAR SYRUP

MAKES 2 CUPS

16 oz (2 cups) sugar

In a small saucepan, bring 16 oz (2 cups) water to a boil. Add the sugar and stir until dissolved.

Remove from the heat and set aside to cool. Pour into a sterilized bottle or jar.

This sugar syrup will keep in the fridge for up to 1 month.

To make Demerara syrup, replace the sugar with demerara sugar.

GRENADINE

MAKES 4 CUPS

4 pomegranates, juiced
(or 32 oz/4 cups pomegranate juice)
16 oz (2 cups) sugar
juice of 1 lemon
1 oz (30 ml) vodka (optional)

In a saucepan over medium-high heat, bring
the pomegranate juice to a boil and simmer until
reduced by half. Add the sugar and stir until
dissolved, then add the lemon juice.

If you wish to store the grenadine for longer than
1 month, add the vodka (it acts as a preservative).

Remove from the heat and set aside to cool.
Pour into a sterilized bottle or jar.

This grenadine will keep in the fridge for up to
1 month, or 3 months with vodka added.

ORGEAT SYRUP

MAKES 4 CUPS

1 lb (450 g) raw almonds, soaked in
warm water for 30 minutes
1½ lb (700 g) sugar
1⅔ oz (50 ml) brandy

Drain the almonds and discard the water.

In a food processor, blend the almonds into a paste,
adding a little water if needed. Transfer to a bowl and cover
with 28 oz (3½ cups) water. Leave to soak for 4 hours.

Strain the almond paste through a cheesecloth (muslin)
lined sieve. Squeeze the cloth to extract the almond oils.
Return the almond paste to the strained water and leave to
soak for another 1–2 hours. Strain and squeeze again.
Repeat the process once more, if desired. Discard the
almond paste.

In a medium-sized saucepan over low heat, gently bring
the almond water to a simmer. Add the sugar and stir
until dissolved. Remove from the heat and set aside
to cool. Stir in the brandy.

Pour into a sterilized bottle or jar. This orgeat syrup will
keep in the fridge for up to 3 months.

*You can substitute hazelnuts, walnuts, pistachios or any
other kind of nut to create delicious syrups that will add
unique flavors to your cocktails.*

HONEY SYRUP

MAKES 2 CUPS

12 oz (350 g) honey

In a small saucepan over medium heat, combine the honey with 8 oz (1 cup) water.

Gradually heat and stir until the honey is dissolved.

Pour into a sterilized bottle or jar. This honey syrup will keep in the fridge for up to 1 month.

*For Rich honey syrup, use 1½ lb (700 g) honey,
or halve the quantity of water.*

VANILLA SYRUP

MAKES 2 CUPS

1 vanilla bean, split open and seeds scraped
16 oz (2 cups) sugar
1 teaspoon vanilla extract

Place the vanilla bean and seeds with the sugar in a saucepan along with 16 oz (2 cups) water. Bring to a boil over medium-high heat and stir until the sugar is dissolved. Stir in the vanilla extract and set aside to cool.

Strain into a sterilized bottle or jar. This vanilla syrup will keep in the fridge for up to 1 month.

CINNAMON SYRUP

MAKES 1 CUP

3 cinnamon sticks
8 oz (1 cup) sugar

Lightly crush the cinnamon into pieces using a mortar and pestle. Transfer to a small saucepan along with the sugar and 8 oz (1 cup) water. Bring to a boil over medium-high heat, stirring until the sugar is dissolved. Set aside to infuse for at least 2 hours.

Strain into a sterilized bottle or jar. This cinnamon syrup will keep in the fridge for up to 1 month.

PASSIONFRUIT SYRUP

MAKES 3½ OZ (105 ML)

pulp from 3 passionfruit
3½ oz (105 g) sugar

Place the passionfruit pulp and sugar in a small saucepan along with 3½ oz (105 ml) water and bring to a boil over medium–high heat. Stir until the sugar is dissolved. Set aside to infuse for at least 2 hours.

Strain into a sterilized bottle or jar. This passionfruit syrup will keep in the fridge for up to 1 month.

VELVET FALERNUM

MAKES 3 CUPS

2 tablespoons blanched slivered almonds
40 cloves, crushed
6 oz (180 ml) white rum
zest of 9 limes
3 inch (7.5 cm) piece fresh ginger, peeled and sliced
12 oz (1½ cups) sugar
1½ oz (45 ml) freshly squeezed lime juice
¼ teaspoon almond extract

In a small dry frying pan over medium heat, toast the almonds and cloves until the almonds are golden. Transfer to a medium-sized sterilized jar along with the rum, lime zest and ginger. Shake vigorously and leave to steep at room temperature for 24 hours.

Strain the rum mixture through a cheesecloth (muslin) lined sieve into a bowl. Squeeze the cheesecloth to get all the oils out of the solids. Discard the solids.

In a clean sterilized jar, combine the sugar with 6 oz (180 ml) warm water and shake until the sugar is dissolved. Add the rum mixture along with the lime juice and almond extract and shake well to combine.

This velvet falernum will keep in the fridge for up to 1 month.

ORANGE BITTERS

MAKES 3 CUPS

24 oz (3 cups) overproof vodka or rum
(50% ABV or higher)
9 oz (250 g) dried orange peel
1 teaspoon fennel seeds
½ teaspoon coriander seeds, lightly crushed
4 cardamom pods, lightly crushed
½ tablespoon gentian root powder (see note)

Combine the ingredients in a sterilized jar and seal.
Store at room temperature for 14 days, shaking
every second day.

Strain through a cheesecloth (muslin) lined sieve
into small sterilized bottles.

The orange bitters will keep indefinitely.

*Gentian root is the bitter root from the gentian plant.
Available from health-food stores or online.*

*If you'd rather not go to the trouble of making your own
bitters, you can purchase flavored bitters from good
bottle shops and specialty liquor stores. Alternately, you
can substitute angostura bitters.*

ALLSPICE DRAM

MAKES 3 CUPS

8 oz (1 cup) white rum
1¼ oz (35 g) allspice berries, lightly crushed
1 cinnamon stick
5½ oz (150 g) soft brown sugar

Combine the rum and allspice berries in a sterilized jar and seal. Store at room temperature for 5 days, shaking every day.

On day 5, break up the cinnamon stick and add to the jar. Steep for another 7 days, shaking every day.

Strain through a cheesecloth (muslin) lined sieve into a clean sterilized jar.

In a small saucepan over medium-high heat, combine the sugar with 12 oz (350 ml) water. Stir until the sugar is dissolved and set aside to cool.

Add the sugar syrup to the rum mixture and shake well to combine.

Leave the allspice dram to rest for at least 2 days before using. It will keep indefinitely.

PEARL DIVER'S MIX

MAKES 4 PORTIONS

¾ oz (20 g) unsalted butter, softened
1½ oz (45 g) honey
1 teaspoon Sugar syrup (page 250)
½ teaspoon Cinnamon syrup (page 255)
½ teaspoon Vanilla syrup (page 254)
½ teaspoon Allspice dram (page 259)

Mix the ingredients together in a small bowl.

This pearl diver's mix will keep for 1 month in an airtight container in the fridge.

COFFEE GROG BATTER

MAKES 4 PORTIONS

1 oz (30 g) unsalted butter, softened
1½ oz (45 g) honey
1 teaspoon Vanilla syrup (page 254)
1 teaspoon Cinnamon syrup (page 255)
½ teaspoon Allspice dram (page 259)

Mix the ingredients together in a small bowl.

This coffee grog batter will keep for 1 month in an airtight container in the fridge.

DON'S MIX

MAKES ABOUT 10 OZ (300 ML)

3½ oz (105 ml) Cinnamon syrup (page 255)
7 oz (210 ml) freshly squeezed grapefruit juice

Mix the ingredients together in a small bowl.

Don's mix will keep for 1 month in an airtight container in the fridge.

COCKTAIL INDEX

Smith Street Books

Published in 2024 by Smith Street Books
Naarm (Melbourne) | Australia
smithstreetbooks.com

ISBN: 978-1-9230-4930-7

Smith Street Books respectfully acknowledges the Wurundjeri People of the Kulin Nation, who are the Traditional Owners of the land on which we work, and we pay our respects to their Elders past and present.

Please note: the recipes from this book have been published in a previous edition of Tiki Cocktails, *first published in 2017.*

Publisher: Paul McNally
Design and illustration: 50s Vintage Dame
Introductory text: Jo Stewart

Printed & bound in China by C&C Offset Printing Co., Ltd.

Book 328
10 9 8 7 6 5 4 3 2 1

MIX
Paper | Supporting
responsible forestry
FSC® C008047